EMERGING TECHNOLOGY ISSUES FOR PEOPLE WITH DISABILITIES

DISABILITY AND THE DISABLED-ISSUES, LAWS AND PROGRAMS

Additional books in this series can be found on Nova's website under the Series tab.

Additional E-books in this series can be found on Nova's website under the E-book tab.

EMERGING TECHNOLOGY ISSUES FOR PEOPLE WITH DISABILITIES

DANIEL B. BERNARDINO
EDITOR

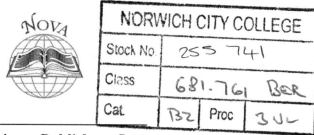

Nova Science Publishers, Inc.
New York

NOTICE TO THE READER

The Publisher has taken reasonable care in the preparation of this book, but makes no expressed or implied warranty of any kind and assumes no responsibility for any errors or omissions. No liability is assumed for incidental or consequential damages in connection with or arising out of information contained in this book. The Publisher shall not be liable for any special, consequential, or exemplary damages resulting, in whole or in part, from the readers' use of, or reliance upon, this material. Any parts of this book based on government reports are so indicated and copyright is claimed for those parts to the extent applicable to compilations of such works.

Independent verification should be sought for any data, advice or recommendations contained in this book. In addition, no responsibility is assumed by the publisher for any injury and/or damage to persons or property arising from any methods, products, instructions, ideas or otherwise contained in this publication.

This publication is designed to provide accurate and authoritative information with regard to the subject matter covered herein. It is sold with the clear understanding that the Publisher is not engaged in rendering legal or any other professional services. If legal or any other expert assistance is required, the services of a competent person should be sought. FROM A DECLARATION OF PARTICIPANTS JOINTLY ADOPTED BY A COMMITTEE OF THE AMERICAN BAR ASSOCIATION AND A COMMITTEE OF PUBLISHERS.

Additional color graphics may be available in the e-book version of this book.

LIBRARY OF CONGRESS CATALOGING-IN-PUBLICATION DATA

Emerging technology issues for people with disabilities / editor, Daniel B. Bernardino.
     p. cm.
   Includes index.
   ISBN 978-1-61122-523-5 (hardcover)
   1. Computers and people with disabilities--United States. 2. Assistive computer technology--United States. 3. Computerized self-help devices for people with disabilities--United States. 4. Accessible Web sites for people with disabilities--United States. 5. Communication devices for people with disabilities--United States. I. Bernardino, Daniel B.
   HV1569.5.E475 2010
   681'.761--dc22
                                                                              2010041308

Published by Nova Science Publishers, Inc. † New York

CONTENTS

PREFACE

There are 54.4 million Americans who have disabilities, and 35 million Americans who have a severe disability. For those aged 15 and over, this includes 7.8 million who have difficulty seeing the words in ordinary newsprint; 7.8 million who have difficulty hearing a typical conversation; 2.5 million who have difficulty having their speech understood; 27.4 million who have lower body limitations; 19 million with upper body limitations; and 16.1 million with cognitive, mental and emotional functioning disabilities. People with vision disabilities still do not have access to all emergency information on video programming or audio access to text messages on the vast majority of cell phones. This book examines the emerging technology issues for people with disabilities, as well as the current challenges and new opportunities

Chapter 1- There are 54.4 million Americans who have disabilities, and 35 million Americans who have a severe disability.[2] For those aged 15 and over, this includes 7.8 million who have difficulty seeing the words in ordinary newsprint; 7.8 million who have difficulty hearing a typical conversation; 2.5 million who have difficulty having their speech understood; 27.4 million who have lower body limitations; 19 million with upper body limitations; and 16.1 million with cognitive, mental, and emotional functioning disabilities.[3]

Chapter 2- The Americans with Disabilities Act (ADA) provides broad nondiscrimination protection in employment, public services, public accommodations, and services operated by private entities, transportation, and telecommunications for individuals with disabilities. As stated in the act, its purpose is "to provide a clear and comprehensive national mandate for the elimination of

However, the ADA, enacted on July 26, 1990, prior to widespread use of the Internet, does not specifically cover the Internet, and the issue of coverage has not been definitively resolved. The Supreme Court has not addressed this issue, although there are some lower court decisions. The cases that directly discuss the ADA's application to the Internet vary in their conclusions about coverage.

Chapter 3 - Statement of Samuel R. Bagenstos, Principal Deputy Assistant Attorney General for Civil Rights, Department of Justice, before the Subcommittee on the Constitution, Civil Rights, and Civil Liberties, Hearing on "Emerging Technologies and the Rights of Individuals with Disabilities."

Chapter 4 - Statement of the American Foundation for the Blind, (Prepared by Mark D. Richert, Esq.), before the Subcommittee on the Constitution, Civil Rights and Civil Liberties, Hearing on "Achieving the Promise of the Americans with Disabilities Act in the Digital Age-Current Issues, Challenges, and Opportunities".

Chapter 5 - Statement of Judy Brewer, Web Accessibility Initiative (WAI) at the World Wide Web Consortium, before the Subcommittee on the Constitution, Civil Rights, and Civil Liberties, Hearing on "Achieving the Promise of the Americans with Disabilities Act in the Digital Age-Current Issues, Challenges, and Opportunities."

Chapter 6 - Statement of Steven I. Jacobs, President, IDEAL Group, Inc., before the Subcommittee on the Constitution, Civil Rights, and Civil Liberties, Hearing on "Achieving the Promise of the Americans with Disabilities Act in the Digital Age-Current Issues, Challenges, and Opportunities".

Chapter 7 - Statement of Daniel F. Goldstein, Esq., Partner, Brown, Goldstein & Levy, LLP, before the Subcommittee on the Constitution, Civil Rights, and Civil Liberties, Hearing on "Achieving the Promise of the Americans with Disabilities Act in the Digital Age-Current Issues, Challenges and Opportunities."

Chapter 8- The technologies used in information and communication products are advancing at an ever increasing rate. Devices are getting smaller, lighter, cheaper, and more capable. Electronics are being incorporated into practically everything, making a wide variety of products programmable, and thus more flexible. Computing power is increasing exponentially. What requires a supercomputer one year can be done on a child's game player 15 years later.

In: Emerging Technology Issues for People...   ISBN: 978-1-61122-523-5
Editors: Daniel B. Bernardino   © 2011 Nova Science Publishers, Inc.

Chapter 1

A GIANT LEAP AND A BIG DEAL: DELIVERING ON THE PROMISE OF EQUAL ACCESS TO BROADBAND FOR PEOPLE WITH DISABILITIES[1]

Federal Communications Commission

I. OVERVIEW

"It seems that all the hard work that we did 20 years ago has virtually disappeared when it comes to updating access standards for broadband and the Internet. Imagine Neil Armstrong watching a re-broadcast 20 years later, in 1989, of his first steps on the moon, only to find his words which echoed across the globe, "one small step for man, one giant leap for mankind," were no longer there – erased, as if he had never been to the moon. That's how taking closed captions out of broadcast content now being shown on the Internet feels to millions of people like myself."

Marlee Matlin
Federal Communications Commission Field Hearing,
Gallaudet University, Washington, D.C., November 6, 2009

There are 54.4 million Americans who have disabilities, and 35 million Americans who have a severe disability.[2] For those aged 15 and over, this includes 7.8 million who have difficulty seeing the words in ordinary newsprint; 7.8 million who have difficulty hearing a typical conversation; 2.5 million who have difficulty having their speech understood; 27.4 million who have lower body limitations; 19 million with upper body limitations; and 16.1 million with cognitive, mental, and emotional functioning disabilities.[3]

Historically, it has taken years – even decades – for these Americans to have anything close to equal access to communications.[4] It took over 100 years for telephone systems to become accessible for people with speech and hearing disabilities; over 50 years for television to become accessible for deaf people; and 10 years for people who used hearing aids to use digital wireless phones.[5] People with vision disabilities still do not have access to all emergency information on video programming or audio access to text messages on the vast majority of cell phones.[6]

Designers of equipment, services and networks have often failed to consider accessibility issues in the design and development stage -- and retrofit solutions are expensive. This has been true for solutions implemented for digital wireless technologies to make them compatible with teletypewriters ("TTYs")[7] and hearing aids. Some would even characterize the FCC's telecommunications relay service ("TRS")[8] as a retrofit solution that was put in place to allow people with hearing and speech disabilities to have access to the public switched telephone network ("PSTN").[9]

Even where consumers with disabilities have made gains in the past, they have often lost these gains with the introduction of new technologies. TTYs and hearing aids that worked with analog cell phones did not work with digital cell phones.[10] Captioning that worked on analog televisions ("TVs") did not work effectively on digital TVs and have largely been omitted from the Internet.[11]

Despite these obstacles, some people with disabilities have been early adopters of technology because it was critical to their economic and educational success.[12] They have been pioneers who have embraced technology and, in the process, have brought gains to all of society. Many technologies that were developed to help people with disabilities gain access have led to technologies that have been later deployed in mainstream products. Voice command technology used to help people with vision, mobility, and cognitive disabilities to type is now being used in cars and e-readers.[13] Predictive-text software, which finishes words that people type in e-mail and search engines, was originally developed as a tool for people with disabilities as well.[14] Closed captioning on video programming, originally designed for people with hearing loss, has become a mainstay in noisy restaurants, airports, and exercise facilities.

With broadband technologies, we have the opportunity to consider accessibility issues relatively early in the deployment process and ensure that people with disabilities share fully in the benefits of broadband. Even more, broadband "bridge[s] gaps and provide[s] opportunities that were inconceivable in the past."[15]

Broadband allows people with disabilities to "live independent lives . . . in their communities of choice."[16] For example, broadband allows people with disabilities to telecommute or run a business out of their home.[17] The National Telecommuting Institute believes that over the next two years it will be able to double the number of people with disabilities it places in in-home jobs (from 400 to 800 annually), and that broadband will be key to its success.[18]

Broadband also makes telerehabilitation services possible, providing long-term health and vocational support to clients in their home communities.[19] These services include teletherapy, telemonitoring, teleconsultation, and the secure exchange of health information among consumers, providers, government, and insurers.[20]

Access to on-line education classes and digital books[21] is also possible with broadband. Readers with print disabilities, for example, can access Bookshare, a searchable online library that offers more than 60,000 digital books, periodicals, and other tools.[22] Volunteers (mostly people who use Bookshare themselves) scan books to make digital books that can be read aloud, enlarged, turned into braille, or spotlighted and read aloud simultaneously.[23]

Broadband also enables people who are deaf or hard of hearing to use video relay service ("VRS"), allowing them to use video phones to communicate with another person through a communications assistant (*i.e.,* relay operator) who is in a remote location via sign language. VRS has been a "life-changing technology" that allows "communicat[ion] with a rapidity and nuance that is not possible with other forms of relay."[24]

For people with autism, on-line technologies have allowed the development of an independent autistic community and culture.[25] One reason is that the challenges associated with interpreting non-verbal and social cues are less significant online.[26] Having the opportunity to connect online with peers also allows people who have autism "to have an understanding that you are not alone in this world."[27]

The promise of broadband for people with disabilities is even greater in the future. For example, E-911 will have real time interoperable voice, video, and text capabilities, allowing equal access to emergency services for people with hearing and speech disabilities,[28] and accessible smart grids will allow people with disabilities to receive information about their electricity, water, and natural gas consumption.[29]

We cannot realize the full potential of broadband, however, unless we fully consider the needs of people with disabilities. As a threshold matter, for example, broadband needs to be defined in a way that recognizes the importance of two-way video capabilities.[30] We also must understand and address the barriers faced by people with disabilities.

This paper will first consider numerous barriers to broadband usage faced by people with disabilities, including inaccessible hardware, software, and services, and inaccessible web content. It will also identify barriers related to specialized assistive technologies that people with disabilities use to gain access to broadband services as well as barriers faced by specific populations within the disability community. Next, the paper will discuss existing private sector efforts to address these barriers, including the advances made by industry innovation and collaborative efforts. It examines how government grant programs and legal and regulatory measures address these barriers as well.

After identifying existing barriers and efforts, this paper next considers the gaps in current efforts to address accessibility for people with disabilities and the needs that must be met if we are to accelerate the adoption path for people with disabilities. Specifically, the government must

- Improve implementation and enforcement of existing accessibility laws;
- Gather and analyze more information about disability-specific broadband adoption issues;
- Coordinate accessibility policy and spending priorities;
- Update accessibility regulations;
- Update subsidy programs and ensure the availability of training and support; and
- Update its approach to accessibility problem solving.

Finally, this paper reviews the three broad recommendations from the National Broadband Plan which seek to address the range of disability access concerns and discusses how the recommendations address the needs identified above. The recommendations include: (1) the creation of a Broadband Accessibility Working Group ("BAWG") within the Executive Branch; (2) the establishment of an Accessibility and Innovation Forum at the FCC; and (3) the modernization of accessibility laws, rules, and related subsidy programs by the FCC, the Department of Justice ("DOJ"), and Congress.

II. TODAY'S BARRIERS

Based on data from its October-November 2009 survey, the FCC estimates that 42% of Americans with disabilities have broadband at home, considerably below the national average of 65%.[31] Some 39% of non-adopters have a disability, much higher than the 24% of the overall survey respondents who have a disability.[32]

People with disabilities face the same major barriers to adoption as other Americans, such as cost of equipment and service, lack of training, and belief that on-line material is not relevant to them.[33] Among non-adopters who have a disability, 37% cited cost as a barrier (compared to 35% of non-adopters without a disability); 25% cited a digital-literacy related topic as their main concern (compared to 19% of non-adopters without a disability); and 17% stated that digital content was not relevant to them (compared to 19% of non-adopters without a disability).[34]

While people with disabilities face many of the same barriers related to costs, digital literacy, and relevance as other Americans, these barriers can sometimes pose additional concerns for people with disabilities. With respect to cost, as detailed below, some people with disabilities must pay for expensive assistive technologies ("AT")[35] in order to access broadband services. Regarding digital literacy, people with disabilities also often do not receive the specialized training and support that they need.[36]

As to relevance, in many cases, people with disabilities are not aware of how broadband could change their lives[37] or that technical solutions exist that would allow them to be broadband adopters.[38] For some, content is not relevant because it is not captioned or described.[39] For others, even when there are technical solutions, they have not always been made available. While VRS is a very relevant broadband application for people who are deaf or hard of hearing, for example, there is no similar speech-to-speech video relay service that would be a compelling broadband application for many people who have speech disabilities.[40]

People with disabilities also face additional barriers not faced by others,[41] including inaccessible hardware, software, services, and content. As mentioned above, AT can be very expensive and presents other challenges as well. In addition, people with disabilities also can have difficulties gaining physical access to libraries and other community-based organizations that provide Internet access.

Inaccessible Hardware, Software, and Services

Mainstream equipment and device manufacturers often do not consider accessibility issues when they design and develop their broadband products, resulting in products that do not have built-in accessibility features and are not compatible with assistive technologies needed by people with disabilities. People with cognitive disabilities or manual dexterity limitations have difficulty with complex and miniaturized menus and user guides;[42] people who are blind cannot use many on-screen menus and touch screens;[43] and people who are hard of hearing cannot use many smart phones and other phone-like devices with their hearing aids.[44]

Mainstream services can also be inaccessible. For example, as people with hearing and speech disabilities have transitioned from using unwieldy, specialized TTYs toward mainstream forms of text and video communications (many of which are IP-based), they no longer have a way to contact E-911 directly.[45] This is because public safety answering points ("PSAPs") very rarely have the capabilities to accept text or video.[46] More generally, most services do not support real time text that is data or IP-based.[47]

Inaccessible Web Pages, New Media Applications, and Video Programming on the Web

Another barrier is that content on the web is often not accessible to people with disabilities. An October 2009 survey of 665 screen reader users suggests that web content is getting more accessible, but the data is mixed: 46.3% think that web content has become more accessible; 33.3% think that web accessibility has not changed; and 20.4% think that web content has become less accessible.[48] The same survey found that only about 8 percent thought that social media sites were "very accessible;" 52 percent found the sites "somewhat accessible;" and about 20 percent found the sites "somewhat inaccessible."[49]

In addition, while there has been recent progress, the vast majority of video programming on the Internet is inaccessible. Most programming, even programming that was originally captioned on traditional television, is not captioned when it is re-shown on the Internet,[50] and video description is virtually non-existent.[51] Furthermore, captioning is proving difficult in the new 3D TV environment as well.[52]

Assistive Technologies That Are Expensive, Not Interoperable with the Latest Technologies, and Difficult to Find

The AT that many people with disabilities need to access broadband can be prohibitively expensive. For example, screen access technology that reads the text that is on the screen for people who are blind or have low vision ranges from between $800-$1,000 for computers and costs approximately $400 for cell phones.[53] Displays that produce the on-screen content in braille cost in the range of $3,500 to $15,000,[54] with an average cost of approximately $5,000.[55] Augmentative and Alternative Communication ("AAC") devices for people with severe motor or other communication disabilities can cost $8,000 or more.[56] While government programs pay for AT under certain circumstances,[57] the European Commission ("EC") recently estimated that people with disabilities in the United States pay for AT out of pocket about 56 percent of the time, which "results in an unmet need among those who cannot afford it."[58]

AT is also often not interoperable with the latest technologies and can be difficult to find, learn how to use, and repair.[59] People with disabilities also have a low awareness of AT products and the benefits that they can provide.[60]

The lack of affordability of AT is probably of the greatest concern to people who are deaf-blind, given the combination of their low incomes and the high cost of the AT that they use.[61] While the price of many kinds of AT has come down dramatically because of innovations in software applications,[62] no such software-based solution exists for the braille display that some in the deaf-blind community require to access broadband services.[63]

Physical Barriers in Libraries and Other Community-Based Organizations

While the focus of the adoption recommendations in the National Broadband Plan is to accelerate the at-home adoption of broadband, the plan also recognizes that libraries and other community-based organizations ("CBOs") are "important venues for free Internet access" and "supportive environments for reluctant and new users to begin to explore the Internet."[64] CBOs that offer computer access, however, may be physically inaccessible to people with disabilities.[65] Nor do they always provide the needed accessible technologies or support.[66]

The table below references some of the most significant barriers to broadband faced by people with disabilities:

Table 1.

Disability	Examples of Significant Broadband Barriers
Vision	• Most devices, menus, and touchscreens do not have text-to-speech/speech-to-text • Expense of screen readers • Lack of website accessibility, including virtually no video description on video programming
Deaf/Hard of Hearing	• Lack of captioning on Internet, including captioning stripped from programming • Lack of direct data or video access to E-911 and general lack of interoperable real time text via data and IP-based technologies • IP-enabled devices are not hearing aid compatible
Deaf-Blind	• Same barriers as above, depending on degree of vision and hearing disabilities • Expense of braille displays and difficulty of getting repairs
Speech	• Expense of AAC devices • Lack of IP-enabled or video assisted speech-to-speech services
Mobility	• Devices and menus that are difficult to manipulate and navigate • Libraries and community centers with computers that are inaccessible
Intellectual	• Devices and menus that are difficult to manipulate and navigate • Lack of training and support
Autism	• Difficult to fully access Internet content without captions or transcriptions • Lack of specialized digital literacy programs

III. ONGOING PRIVATE SECTOR AND GOVERNMENT EFFORTS TO ADDRESS THE BARRIERS

In order to address the barriers set forth above, our efforts must accomplish the following:

- Promote the availability of innovative hardware, software, and services that have built-in accessibility features and standardized interfaces that allow for interoperability between IT and AT;
- Promote the accessibility of web pages, new media content, and video programming on the Internet;
- Promote affordable and innovative AT options and ensure that people with disabilities are aware of these options; and
- Promote training and other support.

This section will discuss ongoing efforts to achieve these objectives. The next sections will discuss the gaps that prevent us from fully achieving these goals and how the National Broadband Plan addresses these gaps.

Ongoing Industry Innovation

Hardware, Software, and Services

Industry innovation and collaborative efforts have tremendous potential to help close the adoption gap among people with disabilities. In the last year, companies have introduced various accessible devices, software, and services. One company introduced a smart phone which contains a built-in screen reader and captioning capabilities.[67] Another introduced a software operating system that supports speech recognition features; a magnifying window; an onscreen keyboard; and a free open-source screen reader.[68] One industry partnership established a real time instant messaging ("IM") relay service, which allows a specially trained relay operator to read IMs to the hearing caller and type IMs dictated by the hearing caller, which are displayed in real time to the end user with a hearing disability.[69]

Companies are also developing Application Programming Interfaces ("APIs") which allow mainstream products to have AT plug-ins from third party developers, often yielding more efficient and affordable accessibility solutions than dedicated AT devices. One application that a consumer can use with a smart phone, for example, allows people with speech and communication disabilities to communicate using natural sounding text-to-speech voices, symbols, and a default vocabulary.[70] The price of the software is about $200, whereas, as mentioned above, a dedicated AAC device can cost $8,000 or more.[71] Some wireless carriers offer accessibility software, such as screen readers, at a significantly discounted rate,[72] and one company offers free downloadable accessibility features for some of its devices, including an application which allows the user to receive short message service ("SMS") messages in braille on a vibrating touchscreen.[73]

Companies, consortia, and individuals are also developing open-source software applications that consumers can download for free.[74] One allows a user to write up to 30 words per minute ("wpm") by pointing or gazing at zooming letters on a screen;[75] another is a screen reader using speech, braille, and magnification;[76] and a third is a program that has both text-to-speech and automatic speech recognition capabilities.[77]

Although recent advances have allowed consumers with disabilities to use software applications to meet their needs, in some cases, dedicated devices or add-on peripherals provide the best accessibility solution. A consumer who is blind, for example, can connect a braille display to a wireless device with an installed global position system ("GPS") application.[78] This technology allows the consumer to navigate in unfamiliar settings and retrieve information about nearby points of interest, such as restaurants, from a database.[79] Other sensoring and monitoring technologies allow seniors and people with disabilities to live more independently in their own communities, for example, by allowing them to push a "help button" which will allow emergency medical personnel and family members to track their location over the Internet.[80]

Public-private partnerships have yielded innovative new hardware solutions as well. The Washington State Office of Deaf and Hard of Hearing ("ODHH") and Humanware, an AT company based in Canada, developed the DeafBlind Communicator ("DBC"), a braille keyboard that connects wirelessly to a cell phone with a screen and keyboard. The DBC allows a person who is deaf-blind to communicate face to face (the other person uses the cell phone key board) or using TTY, SMS, or web browser/e-mail capabilities.[81]

Content

In November 2009, one company announced that it had developed voice recognition technologies which allow viewers of videos on its new media site to request captions.[82] Originally the capabilities applied to videos of a small group of partners, but in March 2010, the company expanded the capability to all videos posted on its site in which there is a clearly spoken audio track in English.[83] Another company has announced plans to launch a free web-based tool that allows individuals to caption any videos from an open video-sharing site.[84] In February 2010, a major television network announced that it will provide closed captions on all of the long form programs that it puts on its online player.[85]

The table below shows some recent innovations that promote accessibility:

Table 2.

Product	Innovation
Smart Phone	Has built-in screen reader and captioning capabilities
Real Time IM Relay Service	Allows relay operator to read instant messages from a caller with a hearing loss to hearing caller in real time and send instant messages to end user with hearing loss in real time
Software Application	Allows user to write up to 30 wpm by pointing or gazing at zooming letters on a screen
Communication Device For People Who Are Deaf-Blind	Braille keyboard that connects wirelessly to a cell phone with a screen and keyboard that allows face to face, TTY, SMS, and web browser/e-mail communications
Voice Recognition Software	Facilitates the captioning of videos on new media site

Ongoing Collaborative Efforts

Hardware, Software, and Services

Industry is also participating in numerous collaborative efforts that promote accessibility. Some are broad efforts, such as the G3ict, a public-private global forum sponsored by the United Nations that is dedicated to facilitating the implementation of the digital accessibility rights defined in the Convention on the Rights of Persons with Disabilities.[86] Several collaborative projects focus on applying universal design principles to mainstream devices, software, and services. One company developed and made public a Universal Design methodology so that wireless equipment and application developers can better create accessible products for their customers.[87] The European Union's ("EU") AEGIS Project, which is funded by the EC and consists of IT industry representatives, disability organizations, research organizations, and universities, identifies user needs and develops open source accessibility solutions for mainstream information and communications technology ("ICT") desktops, web applications, and mobile devices.[88] In addition, REACH112 in the EU is implementing a 12-month pilot project in Sweden, the U.K., the Netherlands, France, and Spain to allow people with disabilities to communicate directly with emergency services with IP devices using voice, video, and text.[89]

Content

Other ongoing efforts focus on making content more accessible. The World Wide Web Consortium's ("W3C") Web Accessibility Initiative, which includes representatives from industry, disability organizations, government, and research labs, has developed and continues to develop strategies, guidelines, and resources to make the web accessible to people with disabilities.[90] The Society of Motion Picture and Television Engineers is working to develop technical standards for the construction of captioning information that accompanies video content distributed over broadband networks and hopes to publish a standard by late 2010.[91]

Assistive Technologies

Other collaborative efforts are also focused on promoting interoperability between information technology ("IT") and AT. The Accessibility Interoperability Alliance ("AIA") is a coalition of IT and AT companies working to enable developers to more easily create accessible software, hardware, and web products.[92] A working group of the International Organization of Standards, ISO/IEC JTC1/SC35/WG6, is seeking to promote broader awareness of open accessibility APIs provided by computer operating systems that allow AT vendors to build hardware and software products that interoperate with mainstream products.[93]

Training

Still other collaborative efforts have focused on training. One company, for example, has "partnered with two non-profit organizations . . . to open 41 centers throughout the United States that provide technology training and assistance for people with a variety of disabilities that affect computer use, such as low vision, hearing loss, and hand and wrist pain."[94] The Cerebral

Palsy Research Foundation, with support from private sector partners and the Departments of Education and Labor, provides computer and workforce training to people with disabilities and low income individuals in Wichita, Houston, New Orleans, and Atlanta.[95]

Ongoing Government Efforts

Numerous government programs promote the adoption of broadband by people with disabilities, either directly or indirectly. The $7.2 billion that Congress appropriated to the Department of Commerce's Broadband Technology Opportunities Program ("BTOP") and the Department of Agriculture's Broadband Infrastructure Program ("BIP") will fund both infrastructure and adoption programs that seek to bring the benefits of broadband to all Americans who are unserved and underserved.[96] The National Council on Disability ("NCD"), an independent federal agency, prepares reports and recommendations for the President, the Congress, and federal agencies on a broad range of disability issues, including technology.[97] In 2006, NCD issued regulatory policy proposals designed to ensure access to communications services by all people with disabilities.[98] Other programs, as discussed below, focus more on specific barriers related to broadband adoption faced by people with disabilities.

Services, Equipment, and Electronic and Information Technology

Many laws, rules, and grant programs serve to promote the accessibility of services and equipment. The TRS program, which was mandated as part of the Americans with Disabilities Act ("ADA"),[99] allows people who are deaf, hard of hearing, and have speech disabilities to have telephone access through a communications assistant ("CA"). Originally, this population communicated through the CAs using a TTY, but now consumers have the option of communicating through the CA via a broadband-based service, such as video relay service or text-based IP relay.

Rules implementing Section 255 of the Communications Act require telecommunications and interconnected Voice over Internet Protocol ("VoIP") manufacturers and service providers to make their products accessible to people with disabilities when it is readily achievable to do so; when it is not, their products must be compatible with AT, if it is readily achievable to do so.[100] FCC rules also require that manufacturers and service providers make a certain percentage of their wireless phone models hearing aid compatible.[101]

And Section 508 of the Rehabilitation Act[102] provides an incentive for electronic and information technology ("EIT") manufacturers and service providers to make their products accessible, because this Section requires the federal government to procure and maintain accessible EIT.[103] In the aftermath of the passage of Sections 255 and 508, the United States Access Board, an independent federal agency that develops accessibility criteria, convened consumer-industry fora to establish accessibility guidelines that would serve as the basis of rules.[104]

The government also provides funding to support universally designed technologies. The Department of Education's National Institute for Disability and Rehabilitation Research, for example, funds a Rehabilitation Engineering Research Center ("RERC") on Universal Interface and Information Technology, which focuses on the accessibility and usability of current and emerging IT.[105] It also funds a Wireless RERC, which works with consumers with disabilities, wireless companies, and researchers to promote access to wireless technologies and the adoption of universal design.[106]

Content

Other rules, laws, and grant programs promote the accessibility of content. Under Section 508, the federal government is required to make its web content accessible to people with disabilities, unless doing so would cause an undue burden.[107] State and local governments also are required under the ADA to provide equal access to their "programs, services, and activities,"[108] and the DOJ's website provides technical assistance to help state and local governments make their web pages accessible.[109]

With respect to video programming, it is not clear whether laws and regulations related to captioning or access to emergency programming apply to programming distributed over the Internet or many IP-enabled devices that play video programming. The Television Decoder Circuitry Act of 1990 requires built-in decoder circuitry to display closed captions and applies to televisions with screens 13" or greater.[110] The captioning regulations promulgated pursuant to provisions passed in the 1996 Telecommunications Act require the captioning of virtually all "video programming."[111]

The government has many ongoing grant programs to promote accessible media. The Department of Education, for example, funds the Described and Captioned Media Program, a program administered by the National Association of the Deaf, which free-loans over 4,000 described and captioned media titles to its members.[112] The National Science Foundation funded work by WGBH's National Center for Accessible Media to produce guidelines for describing science, technology, engineering, and math images in digital talking books and on web sites.[113]

Assistive Technology

Laws requiring equal access for people with disabilities often ensure that people with disabilities have access to AT under certain circumstances. School districts are required to provide AT for students with disabilities where necessary to provide an "appropriate" education under the Individuals with Disabilities Education Act.[114] Public and private employers are generally required to provide AT if necessary as a "reasonable accommodation" to provide equal access to employment opportunities for people with disabilities under the Rehabilitation Act[115] and ADA.[116]

Other programs serve to make AT more affordable for people with disabilities. Medicare, Medicaid, and programs funded by the Veterans' Administration pay for AT under certain circumstances. Although many states have equipment distribution programs that provide AT used to access telecommunications (such as amplified phones or voice activated phones), only Missouri has a program that includes AT used to access the Internet.[117]

Some video relay service providers, who are reimbursed for their "reasonable costs" as part of the FCC's TRS program,[118] provide consumers AT called video phones. Video phones allow relay users to communicate with another person through a communications assistant (*i.e.,* relay operator) who is in a remote location via sign language. Video providers give away phones to entice consumers to use their service,[119] although under our orders, consumer equipment and related expenses are not compensable from the Fund.[120] As part of its recently launched reform efforts,[121] however, the Commission is considering how to make the compensation methodology more fair and efficient and may consider setting up a separate subsidy fund for video phone technologies.

Training

There are also some ongoing training programs at all levels of government. The Department of Defense's Computer/Electronic Accommodations Program is the world's largest AT program and provides AT and training to employees with disabilities at the Department of Defense and throughout the federal government.[122] The Department of Education funds an AT program in the states, which provides a $500,000 grant for training, resources, and rental of a wide range of AT equipment for each state.[123] Assist! to Independence, a non-profit organization in Tuba City, Arizona, which receives some of its funding from the Department of Education, has a Regional Resource Center for Assistive Technology that provides training and education in a range of low-tech and high-tech assistive technologies to the Navajo, Hopi, and Southern Paiute Reservations.[124] The D.C. Public Library has an adaptive technology program[125] that includes online and volunteer in-person assistive technology training for people with disabilities.[126]

The table below provides examples of government programs that address accessibility barriers:

IV. GAPS IN CURRENT EFFORTS

Current public and private efforts have undoubtedly helped to increase broadband penetration among people with disabilities. But there are gaps in our current efforts that we must address, if we are to accelerate the adoption path for people with disabilities. Specifically, the government must

- Improve implementation and enforcement of existing accessibility laws;
- Gather and analyze more information about disability-specific broadband adoption issues;
- Coordinate accessibility policy and spending priorities;
- Update accessibility regulations;
- Update subsidy programs and ensure the availability of training and support; and
- Update its approach to accessibility problem solving.

Table 3

Barrier	Government Program
Service Inaccessibility	Video Relay Service
Content Inaccessibility	Bookshare (funded by Department of Education)
AT Cost	Missouri Telecommunications Access Program for Internet
Lack of Training	D.C. Public Library Adaptive Technology Program

Improve Implementation and Enforcement of Existing Accessibility Laws

Each agency is responsible for its own implementation of Section 508,[127] and implementation has been inconsistent. Agencies often do not focus enough resources on procuring accessible electronic and information technology.[128] In addition, government websites and new media applications continue to pose challenges to people with disabilities.[129]

Section 508 requires the U.S. Office of the Attorney General to submit a biennial report to the President and Congress that provides information on agency compliance and makes recommendations for federal agency accessibility.[130] While the Attorney General prepared an interim report in 2000 also required by the statute,[131] since that time, DOJ has never submitted a biennial report.[132]

Some agencies are also facing challenges applying the requirements of Section 508 of the Rehabilitation Act to new technologies. For example, some federal employers are not providing employees with disabilities access to video relay services or point-to-point communications as reasonable workplace accommodations due to security concerns.[133]

The FCC also needs to improve the enforcement and implementation of its existing accessibility rules, including devoting more resources to outreach. The Commission, for example, has not initiated any enforcement actions with respect to Section 255.[134] This is due in large part to the complexities associated with making a determination as to whether it is readily achievable for a manufacturer or service provider to make a product or service accessible or usable.[135] In the past few years, the Commission has resolved numerous informal Section 255 complaints, and in 2009, it started reporting publicly the number of complaints that it received. But it has undertaken little outreach and has not made public more information about these complaints, such as trends that are reflected in the complaints. The FCC also has not addressed many of the concerns relating to the implementation of captioning rules,[136] which is the area in which the FCC currently receives the greatest number of complaints.[137]

Gather and Analyze More Information about Disability-Specific Broadband Adoption Issues

While the FCC collects some information under the Broadband Data Improvement Act ("BDIA")[138] regarding adoption by people with disabilities, no government entity provides an in-depth analysis of broadband barriers and usage issues relating to different disability subcommunities. Furthermore, while the Department of Commerce released a study on the *entire* AT industry in 2003,[139] the government has never analyzed all the different sources of ICT AT funding, how much each source pays for ICT AT, and how many people with disabilities are not adopters because they have no source of funding for AT that they cannot afford.

This contrasts with the European Commission ("EC"), which did a study analyzing the European ICT AT industry that it released in March 2009.[140] The report also compared the EC's AT delivery system to the one in the U.S.[141] The EC noted that:

> The biggest element to highlight after looking at the U.S. service delivery system for AT is that coverage of assistive technologies is fragmented among a range of programs. Only a few cover a broad range of AT, and many cover only selected technologies as part of broader program objectives . . . This high level of segmentation . . . complicate[s] the ability to determine and provide in a coordinated fashion the specific combination of services and technologiesthat most efficiently and cost-effectively assists individuals in functioning. . .[142]

Coordinate Accessibility Policy and Spending Priorities

The federal government has many programs that contribute directly or indirectly to promoting broadband adoption by people with disabilities, but policies and spending priorities affecting broadband accessibility are not necessarily coordinated across agencies. For example, the DOJ and the FCC need to coordinate on ADA policies that implicate communications policies.

Some program restrictions also may be inconsistent with broader policy objectives. Under Medicare's regulations, for example, coverage of AT is limited to "durable medical equipment" that is "primarily and customarily used to serve a medical purpose" and "generally is not useful to a person in the absence of an illness or injury."[143] This means that Medicare will pay for a dedicated AAC device that costs $8,000 or more but not for a $300 smart phone that can run $150 text-to-speech software and that works more effectively than the AAC device.[144] Policies should promote the development of mainstream technologies with built-in accessibility features and ensure that such technologies can be used to address accessibility needs when it is more efficient and effective to do so.

The government also needs to consider more broadly policies which will promote the development of innovative assistive technologies, lower the cost of AT, and ensure that AT can keep pace and be interoperable with the latest technologies. It should give further consideration to a proposal that the government provide funding for a unified, network-based delivery system for AT, which would lower the cost of AT and provide easy-to-use accessibility features for people with disabilities, seniors, and others who would benefit from simplified access.[145] Under this proposal, software enhancements to the broadband infrastructure would allow people to "call up interface features or adaptations that they need anytime, anywhere, and on any device that they encounter."[146]

The government also needs to consider how to lower the costs of AT by taking full advantage of the relative strengths of different and emerging software development, distribution and licensing models. Government policy and procurement procedures should consider specific aspects and advantages of cloud computing, open source,[147] shared-source and proprietary software. Among the factors that should be considered are costs, innovation, interoperability, distribution, training, and maintenance. The government should also consider how to incentivize states to distribute IT AT to people with disabilities[148] and whether subsidies are needed for AT vendors.[149]

Update Accessibility Regulations

While some in industry who are not regulated are producing accessible products and content because they think it makes good business sense to do so,[150] widespread change and universal access will be more likely if all companies are required to focus on how to make their products accessible. In the past, broadly-based change in the marketplace has not occurred until Congress passed laws or the FCC passed rules mandating accessibility. Access to the PSTN for people with speech and hearing disabilities, captioning, and wireline and wireless hearing aid compatibility only occurred after legislative and regulatory action was taken.

Current accessibility laws and rules often do not cover today's services, equipment, and content. Section 255, for example, applies to telecommunications and interconnected Voice over Internet Protocol ("VoIP") services and equipment but has not been applied to non-interconnected VoIP, electronic messaging, and video conferencing services and equipment. Hearing aid compatibility rules apply to equipment and services that are commercial mobile radio services ("CMRS") but have not been applied to non-CMRS VoIP or other IP-enabled phone-like devices. Rules that mandate captioning capability apply to televisions that are 13" or above (as well as some computer monitors and DTV screens and all DTV tuners and set top boxes) but have not been applied to most other devices that play video programming, including devices that are portable such as smart phones and MP3 players. Captioning rules apply to video programming shown via broadcast, cable, or satellite but have not been applied to programming shown over the Internet.

In addition, the FCC has not engaged in the issue of the need to implement a standard for reliable and interoperable real-time text anytime VoIP is available and supported. In March 2010, however, the Access Board released draft ICT standards and guidelines for Section 255 and Section 508 that include real time text requirements for hardware and software that provides real-time voice conversation functionality.[151]

Furthermore, with respect to commercial websites, DOJ has never clarified the extent to which commercial establishments covered under Title III of the ADA, which protects people with disabilities from discrimination in places of public accommodation, must make their websites accessible. DOJ has indicated in an *amicus* brief and an opinion letter that Title III is applicable to commercial websites,[152] but courts are split on this issue.[153]

Update Subsidy Programs and Ensure the Availability of Needed Training and Support

Current subsidy programs do not provide incentives for the development of AT or mainstream ICT that can promote accessibility. Subsidy programs should ensure that those who cannot afford AT and who do not have access to AT through existing programs have federal support. As mentioned, one population that is particularly in need of specialized devices is the deaf-blind. The American Association of the Deaf-Blind estimates that 4,000 people who do not use broadband now could be online if subsidies were available for braille displays, which have an average cost of about $5,000.[154] The limited size of the relevant population will keep funding requirements small, and federal support is essential to provide the deaf-blind community access to communications as few states are willing to incur the high expenses associated with braille displays.[155]

In addition, government needs to have a comprehensive approach to broadband training and support for people with disabilities. The training should cover the mainstream and assistive technologies used by people with disabilities and use teaching modules that are accessible to people with disabilities, including those with learning and intellectual disabilities.

Update the Approach to Accessibility Problem Solving

The Commission needs to update its approach to accessibility problem solving. This approach needs to recognize the complexity and diversity of the broadband ecosystem[156] and the rapid pace of technological change.[157] The FCC needs to reach out to and engage with all stakeholders on a regular basis, using open and collaborative problem-solving mechanisms. These mechanisms should include an online web presence that uses new media tools to tap into new sources of information and innovation.

V. THE NATIONAL BROADBAND PLAN'S BLUEPRINT FOR ACCESSIBILITY

The National Broadband Plan sets forth specific recommendations to address the gaps identified above and to accelerate the adoption rate for people with disabilities. These recommendations address the barriers faced by all non-adopters as well as the specific accessibility and affordability barriers faced by people with disabilities. This paper also considers additional issues that should be considered in the implementation phase.

There are several broadly-based recommendations that will spur the adoption of broadband by people with disabilities, including the plan's recommendations to make broadband affordable for low-income Americans. For example, the plan recommends that the Universal Service Fund Lifeline and Link-Up telephone support programs be expanded to include broadband.[158]

The plan also recommends the establishment of a digital literacy corps to teach digital literacy skills.[159] The program will be designed to ensure that people with disabilities are fully included – both in terms of content and in terms of accessibility of teaching materials.[160]

In addition, the plan recommends the creation of private partnerships that collaborate with federal agencies that serve low-adopting populations.[161] Under the recommenda-tion, private and non-profit partners would provide discounted hardware and broadband service, as well as relevant software, training and applications, to encourage and enable adoption.[162] Among the agencies cited as ideal potential collaborators is the Social Security Administration, which reaches 7 million children and adults with disabilities who have little or no income and are served by the Supplemental Security Income program.[163]

In addition to addressing barriers that all Americans face, the plan considers the additional affordability and accessibility barriers unique to people with disabilities and provides recommendations to address these barriers.

The plan contains three broad recommendations to address these concerns: (1) the creation of a Broadband Accessibility Working Group ("BAWG") within the Executive Branch;[164] (2) the establishment of an Accessibility and Innovation Forum at the FCC;[165] and (3) the modernization of accessibility laws, rules, and related subsidy programs by the FCC, the Department of Justice ("DOJ"), and Congress.[166]

Broadband Accessibility Working Group

The first major recommendation made in the National Broadband Plan is for the Executive Branch to convene a BAWG.[167] Under the plan, the BAWG would consist of approximately 15 different agencies[168] and "would take on several important tasks."[169] The first of these tasks is to "ensure the federal government complies with Section 508 of the Rehabilitation Act."[170] The plan recommends that the Attorney General prospectively submit the biennial reports required under Section 508, and that the BAWG "work with the Executive Branch to conduct an ongoing and public assessment of the degree to which agencies are complying with Section 508."[171] It also recommends that the BAWG "survey federal agencies to determine how they could apply Section 508 requirements to grant recipients and licensees."[172]

The BAWG would also "coordinate policies and develop funding priorities across agencies."[173] Examples of actions it would take include "identify[ing] and modify[ing] program restrictions preventing new and efficient technologies from being funded" and "exploring whether any public funding should be used for the development and operation of new software enhancements that could support a network-based delivery system for assistive technologies."[174]

In addition, it would "prepare a report on the state of broadband accessibility in the United States within a year after the BAWG is created and biennially thereafter."[175] The report would consider "broadband adoption, barriers, and usage among people with disabilities" and "analyze the root causes of the relatively low broadband adoption rate by people with disabilities and make specific recommendations to address these problems."[176]

The BAWG should also take additional actions consistent with these recommendations. For example, the BAWG should consider how to ensure that as technologies evolve, implementation of Section 508 stays up to date and security and other concerns are addressed.

Accessibility and Innovation Forum

The second major recommendation is that the FCC should establish an Accessibility and Innovation Forum.[177] The forum would "allow manufacturers, service providers, assistive technology companies, third-party application developers, government representatives and others to learn from consumers about their needs, to share best practices, and to demonstrate new products, applications, and assistive technologies."[178] The forum would hold workshops "to share and discuss breakthroughs. . . that promote accessibility" and have an "ongoing Web presence to allow participants to share information about public and private accessibility efforts and discuss accessibility barriers and inaccessible products."[179] The Chairman of the FCC, in conjunction with the forum, "could also present an Accessibility and Innovation Award recognizing innovations" in the public and private sectors "that have made the greatest contribution to advancing broadband accessibility."[180]

The Accessibility and Innovation Forum should be a model of engaged and open government. The web presence should incorporate regular blog coverage, XML feeds for syndication, online video, and crowd-sourcing platforms for harnessing public knowledge and insight. It should also include a clearinghouse of information on the availability of accessible products and services and a list of products and services with access features.[181] In addition, the FCC should undertake outreach through the forum and share specific information about the trends it sees in the complaints it receives. It should also designate a specific contact within the agency through which consumers could request further investigations into potential violations without having to file a formal complaint.

Modernizing Accessibility Laws, Rules, and Subsidy Programs

The third major recommendation is that Congress, the FCC, and DOJ should update accessibility laws, regulations, and related subsidy programs "to cover Internet Protocol-based communications and video programming technologies."[182] The plan notes that H.R. 3101, the Twenty-First Century Communications and Video Accessibility Act of 2009, introduced by Representative Edward Markey, is a starting point for discussion for many of these updates.[183] Specifically, the plan recommends that (1) "the FCC should ensure that services and equipment are accessible to people with disabilities;" (2) "the federal government should take steps to ensure the accessibility of digital content;" and (3) "the FCC should materially support assistive technologies to make broadband more usable for people with disabilities."[184]

Services, Equipment, and Software
With respect to services and equipment, the plan finds that the Commission should "extend its Section 255 rules to require providers of advanced services and manufacturers of end user equipment, network equipment, and software used for advanced services to make their products accessible to people with disabilities."[185] The plan notes that advanced services, as defined in H.R. 3101, include non-interconnected VoIP, electronic messaging, and video conferencing (as well as interconnected VoIP, which is covered by Section 255).[186] The plan also notes that the FCC should "assure itself of its jurisdiction to extend Section 255 to all advanced services or, if it cannot do so, seek authorization from Congress."[187] In addition, the plan notes that H.R. 3101, which requires advanced service providers and equipment manufacturers to make their products accessible unless doing so would cause an undue burden, should be a starting point for discussion of both the scope of coverage and the legal standard of the accessibility obligation applied to service providers and manufacturers.[188]

The plan also recommends that the Commission extend its wireless hearing aid compatibility rules to all types of devices that provide voice communications via a built-in speaker and are typically held to the ear, to the extent that it is technologically feasible.[189] Existing hearing aid compatibility rules require manufacturers and service providers to make a certain percentage of their wireless phone models hearing aid-compatible, but the rules apply only to CMRS phones that connect into the PSTN and utilize an in-network switching facility.[190] Phones using VoIP applications over unlicensed WiFi networks, for example, are typically not covered.[191] In November 2007, the Commission issued a Notice of Proposed Rulemaking in which it sought comment on whether its hearing aid compatibility rules should be modified to address new technologies, including "new devices that more closely resemble mobile computers but have voice communication capability."[192] In this proceeding, the FCC should extend its hearing aid compatibility rules to uncovered service providers and manufacturers of new wireless technologies that provide phone-like capabilities.

In addition, the plan recommends that the Commission open a proceeding on the need to implement a standard for reliable and interoperable real-time text anytime VoIP is available and supported.[193] The Commission should consider the Access Board's draft guidelines on real-time text[194] as part of that proceeding. It should also coordinate its work with Next Generation E-911 efforts to implement a real-time, interoperable voice, video, and text E-911 system.[195] In this endeavor, the Commission should be working to efficiently transition all current users of TTYs to next generation technologies.

Content

With respect to content, the plan recommends that the Commission open a proceeding on "the accessibility of video programming distributed over the Internet; the devices used to display such programming; and related user interfaces, video programming guides, and menus."[196] The inquiry would cover closed captioning decoder and video description capability and the transmission of emergency information over the Internet. The plan also recommends that Congress consider clarifying that the Commission has authority to adopt video description rules and notes that H.R. 3101 should be a starting point for discussion with respect to the scope of the Commission's authority to adopt such rules.[197] The plan also notes that "[a]s part of the proceeding, the Commission should assess its jurisdiction to adopt rules with respect to (i) captioning and emergency information of video programming on the Internet and devices which display such programming and (ii) related user interfaces, video programming guides, and menus."[198]

The inquiry should be a "fact-gathering, analytical initiative to [better] understand the needs of the disabilities community and the contributions that would be required from video service providers, video programmers, manufacturers of end user equipment, software developers, and network providers."[199] It should be coordinated with the ongoing work of the Society of Motion Picture and Television Engineers to "develop technical standards for the construction of captioning information that accompanies video content distributed over broadband networks."[200] It should also be informed by the Consumer Advisory Committee's Working Group on DTV Captioning, and the Commission should assign discrete questions to this group as appropriate.

The plan also recommends that DOJ should amend its regulations to clarify the obligations of commercial establishments under Title III of the ADA[201] with respect to commercial websites.[202] DOJ also should prepare technical assistance on website accessibility for commercial establishments that is similar to the technical assistance it has prepared for state and local governments. In a related matter, DOJ should help localities ensure that libraries and community centers are accessible to people with disabilities by clarifying how localities can meet their obligations under Title II of the ADA[203] and Section 504 of the Rehabilitation Act.[204]

Subsidy Funds

With respect to subsidy funds, the plan recommends that Congress authorize the Commission to use Universal Service Funds ("USF") to provide competitively-based funding to "developers of innovative devices, components, software applications or other AT that promote accessibility."[205] This funding should be capped at $10 million per year.[206] Developers receiving this funding would be eligible to receive the Chairman's Award for Accessibility and Innovation.

The government also should ensure that those who cannot afford AT and who do not have access to AT through existing programs have federal support. Accordingly, the plan recommends that Congress "authorize the FCC to use universal service funds to provide assistive technologies that would enable individuals who are deaf-blind to access broadband services."[207] The plan recommends capping the funding at $10 million per year.[208]

Furthermore, as part of its broader reform efforts,[209] the plan recommends that "the FCC issue an NPRM on whether to establish separate subsidy programs to fund broadband services and AT under the . . . TRS program."[210] Funding is needed because, as mentioned above, while most states fund AT used to access the telephone system, only one state – Missouri – funds assistive technologies used for Internet access.[211] The AT used with TRS include video phones that people with speech and hearing disabilities use to communicate via sign language; braille displays, which connect to a computer and produce a braille output of the text on screen and allow people who are deaf-blind to access IP relay; and captioned phones, which have a screen to display captions of what the other party to the conversation is saying.

The Commission should also consider whether TRS funds should be used to subsidize mainstream technologies that can be used to address accessibility barriers efficiently and effectively. More generally, the Commission should consider how to migrate to a model in which consumers could use a greater number of mainstream technologies to access broadband-based TRS services.[212]

Table 4.

ENTITY	RECOMMENDATION
BAWG	• Ensure government complies with Section 508 • Coordinate funding objectives and policy goals • Issue Biennial State of Accessibility Report
FCC	• Establish Accessibility and Innovation Forum, including clearinghouse • Update Section 255 rules • Update Hearing Aid Compatibility rules • Open proceeding on need for real time text standard for VoIP
	• Open proceeding on accessibility of Internet programming and related devices • Consider TRS funds for subsidies for broadband services and mainstream and assistive technologies • Open rulemaking proceeding on funding Video Assisted Speech-to -Speech as new TRS service
DOJ	• Clarify the applicability of the ADA to commercial websites
CONG-RESS	• Clarify FCC's authority to adopt video description rules • Authorize limited use of USF for AT equipment for people who are deaf-blind and for competitively-based funding for AT developers • Provide FCC authority to update accessibility rules where authority does not exist.

In addition, the plan recommends that the Commission consider providing support for broadband services for low-income people with hearing and speech disabilities,[213] since these services are needed to use IP-based services. The program administrator could use the same criteria as those used under the Lifeline/Link Up program and would only provide funding when no other source of funding was available.[214]

The plan also recommends that the FCC determine "whether additional IP-enabled TRS services, such as Video Assisted Speech-to-Speech Service,[215] could benefit people with disabilities."[216] The Commission should also consider this issue as part of its ongoing reform efforts.

The table below summarizes the recommended actions in the NBP to accelerate adoption by people with disabilities:

VI. CONCLUSION

> [I am] a disabled citizen on a very tight budget . . . I have this computer as a gift from my sister, and I currently have wireless Internet access as part of my rent at the RV park where I live. . . I have difficulty getting out and doing many things physically, and to shop, bank, and the like. . . Before going on line, I rarely socialized because the physical effort to get there, to do so, was just too great. With the Internet, I can do so with little energy output, and enjoy doing so. Believe it or not, that is a big deal.
>   --sandraleesmith46,
>   Posted on Ideascale
>   Broadband.gov, December 19, 2009

Congress has tasked us to "seek to ensure that all people of the United States have access to broadband capability."[217] The International Treaty on the Rights of People with Disabilities, which the United States signed in July 2009,[218] "recognizes the importance of accessibility . . . to information and communication in enabling persons with disabilities to fully enjoy all human rights and fundamental freedoms."[219]

How do we realize this vision and implement a "principle of inclusion"[220] for people with disabilities as we deploy our broadband infrastructure?

We as a society must believe sandraleesmith46 when she tells us that having access to broadband is a big deal. We must embrace the cause and understand that if 39% of non-adopters have a disability, we will not close the adoption gap until we address the barriers faced by people with disabilities. Those barriers may be challenges that are shared with other Americans or they may be barriers that are more disability-specific. Both must be addressed, and, in doing so, we must highlight that accessibility concerns have implications for us all. We must make clear that building-in accessibility at the design and development stage is cost-effective, and that all of society benefits from the widespread use of accessibility features such as captioning, speech recognition, and speech output. An accessible world will even be more important to us as we get older, given the fact that 71% of those 80 or over have a disability.[221]

We also must ensure that government itself is a model of accessibility and that these efforts are part of a larger movement toward open government. We must update our regulations to take into account the new broadband ecosystem. We also must update our *approach* to regulation and foster collaborative and problem-solving processes among stakeholders. Advances in technology must work to close the gap for people with disabilities and not create new barriers that erase the progress of the past. We must build from ongoing public and private efforts but also use new tools and new media to tap into sources of ideas and innovation that were previously unimaginable and unreachable.

Implementing this vision will require ongoing commitment and resources from both the public and private sectors. Indeed, delivering on the promise of equal access to the broadband infrastructure will be one of the "giant leaps" of our generation. Now is the time to engage in this endeavor in earnest and show that we do indeed believe that this is a big deal, for people with disabilities and for all Americans.

End Notes

[1] The author wishes to acknowledge the contributions of those who filed and otherwise participated in the broadband proceeding, from which this paper draws heavily, as well as the contributions of Jamal Mazrui, Erik Garr, Brian David, Elise Kohn, John Horrigan, Greg Elin, Gray Brooks, Kris Monteith, Ellen Satterwhite, Jessica Almond, Krista Witanowski, Joel Gurin, Karen Peltz Strauss, Mark Stone, Yul Kwon, Cheryl King, Thomas Chandler, Amelia Brown, Susan Kimmel, Greg Hlibok, Diane Mason, Scott Marshall, Rachel Kazan, Pam Gregory, Kelly Jones, Helen Chang, Paul de Sa, Zachary Katz, Austin Schlick, Joel Kaufman, Christopher Killion, David Horowitz, Suzanne Tetreault, Colleen Heitkamp, Ruth Milkman, Monica Desai, Jane Jackson, Renee Crittendon, Jeffrey Steinberg, Stagg Newman, Walter Johnston, Salomon Satche, Jennifer Manner, David Furth, Sharon Gillett, Nicholas Alexander, and Richard Hovey of the FCC; and David Capozzi of the Access Board; Daniel Weitzner of the National Telecommunications and Information Administration; Terry Weaver of Government Services Administration; Jennifer Sheehy of the Department of Education; and Samuel Bagenstos and Mazen Basrawi of Department of Justice.

[2] Matthew W. Brault, *Americans with Disabilities: 2005*, CURRENT POPULATION REPORTS 3 (2008) ("2005 Census Report"), http://www.census.gov/prod/2008pubs/p70-117.pdf. The percentage of people who identified themselves as having a disability in this survey is 18.7%, somewhat lower than the 24% who identified themselves as having a disability in the FCC consumer survey discussed *infra*. This variation is due to differences in survey

methodology and context as well as the age range of the respondents. Other sources cite even higher numbers of people with disabilities and functional limitations. The Center for Disease Control and Prevention, for example, states that there are 34.8 million adults who have "hearing trouble" and 25.2 million who have "vision trouble." *See* Centers for Disease Control and Prevention, FastStats: Disability and Functioning (Adults), http://www.cdc.gov/nchs/FASTATS/disable.htm (last visited March 26, 2010).

[3] 2005 Census Report at 6-7.

[4] Rosaline Crawford, Esq. Director, Law and Advocacy Center, ational Association of the Deaf Statement at Broadband Accessibility II Workshop (Oct. 20, 2009).

[5] Karen Peltz Strauss, Co-Chair, Coalition of Organizations for Accessible Technologies Statement at Broadband Accessibility II Workshop (Oct. 20, 2009).

[6] Rehabilitation Engineering Research Center on Telecommunications Access and Communications Service for the Deaf Comments in re NBP PN#25 (*Comment Sought on Transition from Circuit-Switched Network to All-IP Network – NBP Public Notice # 25*, GN Docket No. 09-51, et al., Public Notice, 24 FCC Rcd 14272 (WCB 2009), (*NBP PN# 25*)), filed Dec. 21, 2009, at 2 (RERCTA and CSD Comments).

[7] A teletypewriter or TTY is a type of machine that allows people with hearing or speech disabilities to communicate over the phone using a keyboard and viewing screen. See federal communications commission, connecting america: the national broadband plan 354 (2010) ("National Broadband Plan"), http://www.broadband.gov/plan/.

[8] *See* p. 16, *infra.*

[9] See Karen Peltz Strauss, A New Civil Right, Telecommunications Equality for Deaf and Hard of Hearing Americans 347(Gallaudet Press) (2006) ("Karen peltz strauss, A New Civil Right, telecommunications equality for deaf and hard of hearing americans").

[10] Id. at 387 and 322.

[11] RERCTA and CSD Comments in re NBP PN#25 at 2; Marlee Matlin, National Association of the Deaf Statement at the Broadband Access for People with Disabilities Field Hearing (Nov. 6, 2009).

[12] California Emerging Technology Fund, Accessibility Plan, http://cetfund.org/investments/*accessibility* (last visited Feb. 23, 2010).

[13] Reena Jana, *How Tech for the Disabled Is Going Mainstream,* Business Week, Sept. 24, 2009, http://www.businessweek.com/magazine/content/09_40/b4149058306662.htm.

[14] *Id.*

[15] William E. Kennard and Elizabeth Evans Lyle, With Freedom Comes Responsibility: Ensuring that the Next Generation of Technologies is Accessible, Usable, and Affordable, 10 COMLCON 5, 7 (2001).

[16] World Institute on Disability Comments in re A National Broadband Plan for Our Future, GN Docket No. 09-51, Notice of Inquiry, 24 FCC Rcd 4342 (2009) (National Broadband Plan NOI) at 1-2.

[17] Id.; see also Margaret V. Hathaway, Esq., Vice-President for Public Policy, Spinal Cord Advocates Statement at Broadband Accessibility Workshop II (Oct. 20, 2009) and Alan Hubbard, COO, National Telecommuting Institute, Inc. Statement at the Broadband Access for People with Disabilities Field Hearing (Nov. 6, 2009).

[18] Alan Hubbard, COO, National Telecommuting Institute, Inc. Statement at the Broadband Access for People with Disabilities Field Hearing (Nov. 6, 2009).

[19] Katherine D. Seelman, Ph.D., Professor, Rehabilitation Science and Technology, University of Pittsburgh Statement at Broadband Accessibility II Workshop (Oct. 20, 2009).

[20] Id.

[21] World Institute on Disability Comments in re National Broadband Plan NOI at 1 and Fruchterman (Benetech) Statement at Broadband Accessibility Workshop II (Oct. 20, 2009).

[22] Bookshare, Books without Barriers, *http://www.bookshare.org/* (last visited Feb. 12, 2010). A print disability is one that "makes it difficult or impossible to read a printed book," and

includes vision, physical, and learning disabilities. See id. Bookshare receives funding from the Department of Education and other donors.

[23] Jim Fruchterman, President, Benetech Statement at Broadband Accessibility Workshop II (Oct. 20, 2009).

[24] Letter from I. King Jordan, President Emeritus Gallaudet University, to Marlene H. Dortch, Secretary, FCC, CG Docket No. 03-123 (May 19, 2009) at 1.

[25] Ari Ne'eman, Founding President, Autistic Self Advocacy Network Statement at the Broadband Access for People with Disabilities Field Hearing (Nov. 6, 2009) (Ne'eman Statement).

[26] Id.

[27] Id.

[28] Patrick Halley, Director, Government Affairs, National Emergency Number Association Statement at the Broadband Access for People with Disabilities Field Hearing (Nov. 6, 2009).

[29] Ishak Kang, CEO/Founder, dot UI Statement at Broadband Accessibility Workshop II (Oct. 20, 2009).

[30] For an effective video quality necessary for a two-way conversation, upload and download speeds will need to be equally robust to support the application's demands in both directions. See THOR KENDALL, THE BROADBAND AVAILABILITY GAP (OBI Working Paper, forthcoming 2010).

[31] JOHN B. HORRIGAN, BROADBAND ADOPTION AND USE IN AMERICA 3 (FEDERAL COMMUNICATIONS COMMISSION) (2010) ("Horrigan Adoption Paper").

[32] Id.

[33] Id. at 30.

[34] Horrigan Adoption Paper at 38.

[35] Assistive technologies encompass a wide range of products used to "maintain, increase, or improve the functional capabilities of people with disabilities." Assistive Technology Act of 1998, as amended, Pub. L. No. 108-364, 118 Stat. 1707 (2004). With respect to devices and software needed for Internet access, assistive technologies include such things as "screen reading software, screen enlarging, alternative key boards, alternative mice, pointing devices, and braille [displays]." C. Marty Exline, Director, Missouri Assistive Technology Program Statement at the Broadband Accessibility Workshop II (Oct. 20, 2009).

[36] See, e.g., American Council of the Blind Comments in re: NBP PN #4, (Comment Sought on Broadband Accessibility for People with Disabilities Workshop II: Barriers, Opportunities, and Policy Recommendations—NBP Public Notice #4, GN Docket Nos. 09-47, 09-51, 09-137, Public Notice, 24 FCC Rcd 11968 (CGB 2009)) (NBP PN #4)), filed Oct. 7, 2009, at 2; Elizabeth Weintraub, Member, Council on Quality and Leadership Statement at Broadband Accessibility II Workshop (Oct. 20, 2009); and Ne'eman Statement.

[37] See Connected Nation Comments in re NBP PN # 4 filed Oct. 6, 2009, at 1 (finding that 40 percent of people with disabilities who had not adopted broadband said that they had no need for broadband).

[38] Rehabilitation Engineering Research Center on Universal Interface and Information Technology Access Comments in re NBP PN # 4, filed Oct. 6, 2009, at 13.

[39] See Larry Goldberg, Director, Media Access Group at Statement at the Broadband Accessibility II Workshop (Oct. 20, 2009) ("Accessible online media is the killer app for . . . [the disability] community, and far too little is available today.")

[40] Rebecca Ladew, East Coast Representative, Speech Communications Assistance by Telephone, Inc. Statement at Broadband Accessibility II Workshop (Oct. 20, 2009) (stating the need to expand the Commission's Telecommunications Relay Service to include a program which would allow people with speech disabilities to use video-assisted speech over broadband to communicate through a communications assistant trained in understanding people with speech disabilities, who would then relay the call to anyone on the PSTN).

[41] This is not to say that only people with disabilities would benefit if these barriers were addressed. Research sponsored by Microsoft, for example, shows that "nearly six out of 10 adult computer users [are] in a position to benefit from some sort of accessibility feature." Letter from Paula Boyd, Regulatory Counsel, Microsoft Corporation, to Marlene H. Dortch, Secretary, FCC, GN Docket Nos. 09-47, 09-51, 09-137 (Dec. 2, 2009) ("Microsoft December 2, 2009 Ex Parte") at 5.

[42] Karen Peltz Strauss, *Past and Present: Making the Case for a Regulatory Approach to Addressing Disability Discrimination in the Provision of Emerging Broadband and Cable Technologies,* BROADBAND AND CABLE TELEVISION LAW 2010, DEVELOPMENTS IN CABLE TECHNOLOGY, PRACTISING LAW INSTITUTE at 5, Jan. 26, 2010 (*"Strauss PLI Paper")* http://trace.wisc.edu/docs/2010-broadband-cable-regs/.

[43] See, e.g., Eric Bridges, American Council of the Blind Statement at Broadband Accessibility Workshop II (Oct. 20, 2009) (noting that the first smart phone that had built-in features allowing it to be used by a person who was blind was introduced in July 2009) and National Federation of the Blind Comments in re NBP PN #4 filed Oct. 6, 2009, at 4.

[44] See, e.g., Strauss PLI Paper at 16.

[45] See Comments of Telecommunications for the Deaf and Hard of Hearing, Inc. in re NBP #14 (Comment Sought on Public Safety Issues Related to Broadband Deployment in Rural and Tribal Areas and Communications to and from Persons with Disabilities, GN Docket No. 09-51, et al., Public Notice, 24 FCC Rcd 13512 (WCB 2009)), filed Dec. 1, 2009, at 2.

[46] Id.

[47] Real-time text differs from traditional forms of text communications such as text messaging, in that it provides an instantaneous exchange, character by character, whereas traditional forms of text-communications such as text messaging require users to finish their typed message before sending it. See Strauss PLI Paper at 17.

[48] WEBAIM SCREEN READER USER SURVEY RESULTS (2009), available at *http://www.web aim.org/projects/screenreadersurvey2/*

[49] Id.

[50] Rehabilitation Engineering Research Center on Telecommunications Access Comments in re NBP PN#4, filed Oct. 6, 2009, at 3.

[51] Id. Video description is "the insertion of verbal descriptions of on-screen visual elements during natural pauses in a program's audio content." Strauss PLI Paper at 6, n. 17 (2010).

[52] Vioditv, 3DTV Not Quite Ready for Primetime, http://www.viodi.tv/2010/01/10/3dtv-not-quite-ready-for-prime-time/ (last visited Feb. 25, 2010).

[53] National Federation of the Blind Comments in re NBP PN # 4, filed Oct. 6, 2009, at 3.

[54] American Foundation for the Blind, Technology - Assistive Technology - Braille Technology, *http://www.afb.org/Section.asp?SectionID=4&TopicID=31&DocumentID=1282* (last visited Jan. 9, 2010).

[55] Elizabeth Spiers, in re A Few More Questions, BLOGBAND, *http://blog.broadband.gov/?entryId=10743#comments.*

[56] Ashlee Vance, Insurers Fight Speech-Impaired Remedy, THE NEW YORK TIMES, Sept. 15, 2009, *http://www.nytimes.com/2009/09/15/technology/15speech.html?_r=1&scp=1&sq=impairm ent&st=cse.*

[57] See discussion at pp. 17-18, infra.

[58] See EUROPEAN COMMISSION, ANALYSING AND FEDERATING THE EUROPEAN ASSISTIVE TECHNOLOGY ICT INDUSTRY 38-41 (2009) ("2009 EC Report"), *http://ec.europa.eu/information_society/newsroom/cf/itemlongdetail.cfm?item_id=4897*

[59] See, e.g., Karen Peltz Strauss, Co-Chair, Coalition of Organizations for Accessible Technology Statement at the Broadband Access for People with Disabilities Field Hearing (Nov. 6, 2009) and Elizabeth Spiers, Director, Information Services, American Association of the Deaf-Blind Statement at the Broadband Access for People with Disabilities Field Hearing (Nov. 6, 2009). See also National Council on Disability, Federal Policy Barriers to Assistive

Technology, Stakeholder Validation Section (unpaginated) (2000), *http://www.ncd.gov/newsroom/publications/2000/assisttechnology.htm#1* (finding in survey of 2000 AT users that biggest AT-related barriers were lack of information about the appropriate AT and lack of funds for AT).

[60] Microsoft Dec. 2, 2009 Ex Parte at 4.

[61] Rehabilitation Engineering Research Center on Telecommunications Access Comments in re NBP PN # 4, filed Oct. 6, 2009, at 2-3.

[62] See, e.g., Letter from K. Dane Snowden, Vice President, External and State Affairs, CTIA - the Wireless Association, to Marlene H. Dortch, Secretary, FCC, GN Docket Nos. 09-47, 09-51, 09-147 (November 16, 2009) (CTIA Nov. 16 Ex Parte) at 5. See also infra at p. 11-12.

[63] For some in the deaf-blind community, having a braille display is also the most efficient way to access basic telephone service (through IP-based TRS services). See Elizabeth Spiers, in re A Few More Questions, BLOGBAND, *http://blog.broadband.gov/?entryId=10743#comments.*

[64] National Broadband Plan at 176.

[65] U.S. BROADBAND COALITION, BROADBAND ADOPTION AND USE: BRIDGING THE DIVIDE AND INCREASING THE INTENSITY OF BROADBAND USE ACROSS ALL SECTORS OF THE ECONOMY 22 (2009), *http://www.baller.com/pdfs/US_Broadband_Coalition_AandU_Report_11-13-09.pdf*.

[66] Id.

[67] Apple, Apple's Commitment to Accessibility, *http://www.apple.com/accessibility* (last visited Feb. 11, 2010).

[68] Microsoft, Window's 7 features, *http://windows* (last visited Feb. 11, 2010).

[69] AT&T Comments in re NBP PN # 4, filed Oct. 6, 2009, at 1.

[70] CTIA Nov. 16 Ex Parte at 5 (citing Proloquo2Go application that can be used with the Apple i-phone).

[71] See n. 47, supra.

[72] CTIA Comments in re NBP PN #4, filed Oct. 6, 2009, at 6-7.

[73] CTIA Nov. 16 Ex Parte at 4 (citing Nokia's "Braille Reader").

[74] Letter from Christopher Hankin, Senior Director, Global Communities, Sun Microsystems, to Marlene H. Dortch, Secretary, FCC, GN Docket No. 09-51(Nov. 23, 2009) at 1.

[75] See Dasher Project: Special Needs, *http://www.inference.phy.cam.ac.uk/dasher/SpecialNeeds.html* (last visited Feb. 11, 2010).

[76] See Live.gnome.org, About Orca, *http://live.gnome.org/Orca* (last visited Feb. 11, 2010). Orca runs on the GNOME desktop and its development has been led by the Accessibility Program Office of Sun Microsystems.

[77] See Dimio, D-Software by Dimio, *http://dimio.altervista.org/eng/* (last visited Feb. 11, 2010).

[78] Robert D. Atkinson and Daniel D. Castro, Digital Quality of Life: Understanding the Personal and Social Benefits of the Information Technology Revolution 51 (Information Technology & Innovation Foundation) (2008), *http://www.itif.org/index.php?id=179.*

[79] Id.

[80] See Silvers Summit Technology for Life, Mobile Help: Cellular and GPS-Enabled Mobile Personal Emergency Response System (M-Pers), *http://silverssummit.com/index.php?option=com_myblog&show=iPhone-Health-Applications.html&Itemid=5* (last visited Apr. 23, 2010).

[81] Humanware, DeafBlind Communicator: Opening Doors to the World, *http://www.humanware.com/en-usa/products/blindness* (last visited Apr. 23, 2010).

[82] *Broadcasting* Ourselves ;), The Official YouTube Blog, The Future Will Be Captioned: Improving Accessibility on YouTube, March 4, 2010, *http://youtube-global.blogspot.com/2010/03/future-will-be-captioned-improving.html.*

[83] Id.

[84] Matthew Knopf, Vice President, Business Development, PLYmedia Statement at the Broadband Accessibility II Workshop (Oct. 20, 2009).

[85] See Blair Levin (FCC), Marlee and Mickey, BLOGBAND, February 22 , 2010, *http://blog.broadband.gov/?category=Disabilities%20Access*.

[86] G3ict, About G3ict, *http://g3ict.com/about* (last visited Feb. 11, 2010). The United Nations ratified the Convention in December 2006. President Obama signed the convention in July 2009, but it has not been ratified by the Senate.

[87] AT&T Comments in re NBP PN # 4, filed Oct. 6, at 1.

[88] AEGIS Project, "About AEGIS," *http://www.aegis-project* (last visited Feb. 11, 2010).

[89] REACH112, What is REACH112? *http://www.reach112.eu/view/en/index.html* (last visited Feb. 11, 2010).

[90] W3C, Accessibility, *http://www.w3.org/standards/webdesign/accessibility* (last visited Feb. 11, 2010).

[91] Society of Motion Picture and Television Engineers Comments in re NBP PN #4, filed Oct. 6, 2009, at 2.

[92] Peter Abrams, Accessibility Interoperability Alliance News, IT Analysis Communications Ltd., September 1, 2008, *http://www.it-director.com/business/compliance*.

[93] ISO/IEC, JTC1/SC35/WG6 - User Interface Accessibility, *http://www.open-std.org/Jtc1/SC35/wg6/* (last visited Feb. 11, 2010).

[94] Microsoft Dec. 2, 2009 Ex Parte at 9.

[95] Janis Krohe, Ph.D., VP, Employment Services Division, Cerebral Palsy Research Foundation Statement at the Broadband Access for People with Disabilities Field Hearing (Nov. 6, 2009).

[96] See Daniel Weitzner, Associate Administrator for the Office of Policy Analysis and Development, Department of Commerce, NTIA Statement at the Broadband Accessibility II Workshop (Oct. 20, 2009) and Gary Bojes, Ph.D., Senior Level Program and Policy Advisor, Rural Utility Service, U. S. Department of Agriculture Statement at the Broadband Accessibility II Workshop (Oct. 20, 2009).

[97] National Council on Disability, NCD Publications by Subject, *http://www.ncd.gov/newsroom/publications/index_subject.htm* (last visited March 14, 2010).

[98] National Council on Disability, The Need for Federal Legislation and Regulation Prohibiting Telecommunications and Information Services Discrimination, Dec. 19, 2006, *http://www.ncd.gov/newsroom/publications/2006/discrimination*

[99] The Americans with Disabilities Act of 1990, Pub. L. No. 101-336, 104 Stat. 327 (1990) (codified at 47 U.S.C. §225) ("ADA Title IV").

[100] See 47 C.F.R. § 6.1 et seq.

[101] See 47 C.F.R. § 20.19.

[102] Workforce Investment Act of 1998, Pub. L. No. 105-220, 112 Stat 936 (1998) (codified at 29 U.S.C. § 794d) ("WIA Section 508").

[103] Under Section 508 of the Rehabilitation Act, federal agencies must "develop, procure, maintain, and use" electronic and information technologies that are accessible to people with disabilities – unless doing so would cause an "undue burden." WIA Section 508 (a)(1)(A).

[104] United States Access Board, Guidelines and Standards, *http://www.access-board.gov/gs.htm* (last visited Feb. 12, 2010).

[105] Trace Center, "RERC on Universal Interface and IT Access," *http://trace.wisc.edu/itrerc/* (last visited Feb. 12, 2010).

[106] Wireless RERC, About Us, *http://www.wirelessrerc.org/about-us* (last visited Feb. 12, 2010).

[107] WIA Section 508 (a)(1)(A).

[108] ADA Title IV, (codified at 42 U.S.C. § 12101).

[109] U.S. Department of Justice, Accessibility of State and Local Government Websites to People with Disabilities, *http://www.ada.gov/websites2_prnt.pdf* (last visited Feb. 12, 2010).

[110] The Television Decoder Act Circuitry Act of 1990, Pub. L. No. 101-431, 104 Stat. 960 (1990) (codified at 47 U.S.C. § 303 (u) and § 330(b)). Subsequently, the Commission amended its rules to require captioning capability in computer monitors that are 13" or greater in diameter; digital television (DTV) screens measuring 7.8" or greater vertically; and all standalone DTV tuners and set top boxes, regardless of size. See Strauss PLI Paper at 11.

[111] The Commission defines "video programming" as "[p]rogramming provided by, or generally considered comparable to programming provided by, a television broadcast station that is distributed and exhibited for residential use." 47 C.F.R. § 79.1(a)(1).

[112] Described and Captioned Media Program, About Us, *http://www.dcmp.org/About/Default .aspx* (last visited Feb. 12, 2010).

[113] National Center for Accessible Media, WGBH's National Center for Accessible Media Publishes Free Guidelines for Describing STEM Images for Use within Digital Talking Books and on Web Sites (press release), Sept. 24, 2009, available at *http://ncam.wgbh.org/about/news/ncam-publishes-guidelines* .

[114] Individuals with Disabilities Education Act, as amended in 2004, Pub. L. No. 108-446, 118 Stat. 2647 (2004).

[115] Rehabilitation Act of 1973, Pub. L. No. 93-112, 87 stat. 355, §504 (1973). Section 504 of the Rehabilitation Act requires that programs and activities conducted or funded by the federal government be accessible to people with disabilities where doing so would not create an undue burden.

[116] See ADA, supra n. 99.

[117] C. Marty Exline, Director, Missouri Assistive Technology Program Statement at the Broadband Accessibility Workshop II (Oct. 20, 2009).

[118] Telecommunications Relay Services and Speech-to-Speech Services for Individuals with Hearing and Speech Disabilities, CC Docket No. 90-571, Report and Order, Order on Reconsideration, and Further Notice of Proposed Rulemaking, 19 FCC Rcd 12475, 12551, para. 199 (2004).

[119] Letter from Claude Stout, Executive Director, Telecommunications for the Deaf and Hard of Hearing, Inc., to Marlene H. Dortch, Secretary, FCC, GN Docket 09-51 (Nov. 17, 2009) at 4.

[120] Telecommunications Relay Services and Speech-to-Speech Services for Individuals with Hearing and Speech Disabilities, CG Docket 03-123, Report and Order and Declaratory Ruling, 22 FCC Rcd 20140, 20170-20171, para. 82 (2007).

[121] These efforts are focusing on: (i) fraud and abuse; (ii) the most efficient way to deliver VRS while maintaining functional equivalency; and (iii) a fair and transparent compensation methodology. See FCC Announces Agenda and Panelists for Workshop on VRS Reform To Be Held on December 17, 2009, Press Release, (CGB Dec. 15, 2009), available at *http://hraunfoss.fcc.gov/edocs_public/attachmatch/DOC-295208A1.doc*.

[122] Computer/Electronic Accommodations Program, CAP Timeline and History, *http://www.tricare.mil/CAP/About_us/CAP_Timeline.cfm*, (last visited Feb. 28, 2010).

[123] Department of Education, Assistive Technology, *http://www2.ed.gov/programs/atsg /index. html* (last visited Feb. 12, 2010).

[124] ASSIST! to Independence, Helping American Indians with differing abilities live in harmony, *http://www.assisttoindependence.org/index.html* (last visited Feb. 12, 2010).

[125] Adaptive technologies are "a type of assistive technology that includes customized systems that help individuals move, communicate, and control their environments." Family Center on Technology and Disability, FCTD AT Fact Sheet Services: Assistive Technology Glossary, *http://www.fctd.info/show/glossary*, (last visited Feb. 12, 2010).

[126] Patrick Timony, Adaptive Technology Coordinator, DC Public Library Statement at the Broadband Access for People with Disabilities Field Hearing (Nov. 6, 2009).

[127] See n. 116, supra.

[128] See, e.g., Eric Bridges, American Council of the Blind Statement at the Broadband Accessibility Workshop II (Oct. 20, 2009) (stating that the Veterans' Administration

Section 508 compliance office evaluates about 300 IT projects on a budget of less than $1 million per year).

[129] See, e.g., Karen Peltz Strauss, Co-Chair, Coalition of Organizations for Accessible Technologies Statement at the Broadband Accessibility Workshop II (Oct. 20, 2009) and Alice Lipowicz, "Federal sites rapped over accessibility problems," FEDERAL COMPUTER WEEK, Oct. 23, 2009, *http://www.fcw.com/Articles/2009/10/26/Week-Section-508-recovery.aspx*

[130] WIA § 508(d)(2).

[131] WIA § 508(d)(1)

[132] See Department of Justice, Civil Rights Division, Section 508 Homepage, *http://www.justice.gov/crt/508/508home.php* (last visited Jan. 16, 2010).

[133] See KAREN PELTZ STRAUSS, VIDEOTELEPHONY AND VIDEO RELAY SERVICE POLICIES AFFECTING U.S. FEDERAL EMPLOYEES WITH COMMUNICATION DISABILITIES: AN ANALYSIS 6-9 (ITU-T Workshop) (2009), *http://www.itu.int/dms_pub/itu-t/oth/06/28/ T062800000600222PDFE.pdf*. Section 501of the Rehabilitation Act also requires non-discrimination in employment by Federal agencies. See Rehabilitation Act of 1973, supra n. 128, at § 501.

[134] This contrasts to its enforcement of the wireless hearing aid compatibility requirements, where it has been active. See Enforcement Bureau Takes Action to Enhance Access to Digital Wireless Service for Individuals with Hearing Disabilities, Public Notice, 25 FCC Rcd 370 (EB 2010).

[135] The three formal complaints that consumers have filed have all settled without a determination being made as to how to enforce the "readily achievable" standard. *See* Dr. Bonnie O'Day v. Cellco Partnership d/b/a Verizon Wireless, Motion To Dismiss With Prejudice, EB-03-TC-F-001, Order, 19 FCC Rcd 17477 (2004); Frank Winsor Burbank and Barbara Gail Burbank v. OnStar Corporation, EB-03-TC-F-001, Order, 19 FCC Rcd 16652 (2004); and Dr. Bonnie O'Day v. Audiovox Communications Corporation, EB-03-TC-F-004, Order, 19 FCC Rcd 14 (2004).

[136] These concerns include addressing a 2004 petition that the Commission adopt specific quality requirements for captioning and addressing hundreds of "undue burden" petitions from religious non-profits and others, who do not have to caption their programming while their petitions are pending before the Commission. See Letter from Nguyen T. Vu, Counsel to Telecommunications for the Deaf and Hard of Hearing, Inc., to Marlene H. Dortch, CG Docket No. 03-123, (March 2, 2009), Attachment at 3.

[137] For example, in the first quarter of 2009, 142 of the total 226 informal complaints concerned captioning. See FCC News, Report on Informal Consumer Complaints Regarding Access to Telecommunications for People with Disabilities," Press Release,(CGB Sept. 8, 2009) available at *http://hraunfoss.fcc.gov/edocs_public/attachmatch/DOC-293274A1.doc*.

[138] Broadband Data Improvement Act of 2008, Pub. L. No. 110-385, 122 Stat. 4097 (2008) (codified at 47 U.S.C. §§ 1301-04) ("BDIA"). Section 103(c) of the BDIA provides that the Commission conduct a periodic consumer survey of broadband service capability.

[139] According to the Department of Commerce survey, only 9% of the U.S. assistive technology companies focused on products related to computers (as compared to, for example, 20.7% for mobility; 12.2% for orthotics/prosthetics; 12.0% for aids to daily living; and 10.4% for communication devices). See U.S. DEPARTMENT OF COMMERCE, BUREAU OF INDUSTRY AND SECURITY, TECHNOLOGY ASSESSMENT OF THE U.S. ASSISTIVE TECHNOLOGY INDUSTRY 7-8 (2003), *http://www.icdr.us/atreportweb/index.htm*

[140] 2007 EC Report.

[141] The report noted that the U.S. differed from the EC in that its assistive technology programs were for the most part rooted in universal design and anti-discrimination laws, rather than direct subsidies for the end user. See id. at 7. The report recommends that the ICT AT industry in the European Union ("EU") would be strengthened if industry formed a

federation or other type of ICT AT industry association, similar to the Assistive Technology Industry Association in the United States. Id. at 139.

[142] Id. at 41.

[143] See 42 C.F.R. § 414.202.

[144] See Ashlee Vance, Insurers Fight Speech-Impaired Remedy, THE NEW YORK TIMES, September 15, 2009, *http://www.nytimes.com/2009/09/15/technology/15speech.html?_r=1&scp=1&sq=impairm ent&st=cse*. Medicare will pay for a separate software application that performs the function, but not for hardware, even if the hardware has built-in software that provides the function. See Centers for Medicare and Medicaid Services, Medicare Coverage Determinations Manual, Chapter 1, Part 1, Section 50.1, *http://www.cms.hhs.gov/ manuals/ downloads/ncd103c1_Part1.pdf*.

[145] See Letter from Gregg Vanderheiden, Director, RERC on Universal Interface and Information Technology Access, Trace R&D Center, Univ. of Wisconsin; Jim Fruchterman, President, Benetech; Larry Goldberg, Director, Carl and Ruth Shapiro National Center for Accessible Media at WGBH (NCAM); Dale Hatfield, ICT Consultant, former Chief Engineer, FCC; Eve Hill, Burton Blatt Institute; Karen Peltz Strauss, Principal, KPS Consulting; and Jim Tobias, President, Inclusive Technologies, to Marlene H. Dortch, Secretary, FCC, GN Docket Nos. 09-47, 09-51, 09-137 (Jan. 6, 2010) at 1.

[146] Karen Peltz Strauss, Co-Chair, Coalition of Organizations for Accessible Technology Statement at the FCC Field Hearing on Broadband Access for People with Disabilities, Nov. 6, 2009. Under the proposal, "the basic structure, tools, resources, and security for the development and support of a variety of access products and features" would be publicly funded and the "ecosystem for accessibility products and features consisting of commercial assistive technology (AT) companies, mainstream ICT companies, free and open source developers, and [others]" would mostly be privately funded. Id.

[147] See Letter from Christopher Hankin, Senior Director, Global Communities, Sun Microsystems, to Marlene H. Dortch, Secretary, FCC, GN Docket No. 09-51 (Nov. 23, 2009) at 1.

[148] Currently, Missouri is the only state that distributes assistive technologies that are used to access the Internet. See C. Marty Exline, Director, Missouri Assistive Technology Program Statement at the Broadband Accessibility Workshop II (Oct. 20, 2009).

[149] See Letter from Paula Boyd, Regulatory Council, Microsoft Corporation, to Marlene H. Dortch, Secretary, FCC, GN Docket Nos. 09-47, 09-51, 09-137 (Dec. 2, 2009) at 10.

[150] See, e.g., Microsoft December 2, 2009 Ex Parte at 5; Ken Salaets, Information Technology Industry Council in re A Few More Questions, *http://blog.broadband. gov/? entryId=10743#comments*; and Tom Krazit, Web Accessibility No Longer an Afterthought, CNET NEWS, Dec. 14, 2009, *http://news.cnet.com/8301-30684_3-10414041-265.html*.

[151] See United States Access Board, Draft Information and Communication Technology (ICT) Standards and Guidelines, (March 2010) at 80, ("Access Board Draft Guidelines"), http://www.access-board.gov/sec508/refresh/draft-rule.pdf.

[152] See Hooks v. Okbridge, No.99-50891 (5th Cir. 1999), Brief of the United States as Amicus Curiae in Support of Appellant and Letter to Senator Tom Harkin from Deval L. Patrick, Assistant Attorney General, Civil Rights Division, United States Department of Justice (Sept. 9, 1996).

[153] Cf, e.g., National Federation of the Blind v. Target Corp., 452 F. Supp. 2d 946, 956 (N.D. Cal. 2006) (holding that Article III of the ADA is applicable "if the inaccessibility of the website impedes the full and equal enjoyment of goods and services in the [store itself]") to Access Now, Inc. v. Southwest Airlines, Co., 227 F. Supp. 2d 1312 (S.D. Fla. 2002) (holding that an airline Internet website is not a "place of public accommodation" within the meaning of Title III of the ADA).

[154] Elizabeth Spiers, in re A Few More Questions, BLOGBAND, *http://blog.broadband.gov/? entryId=10743#comments*

[155] Strauss PLI Paper at 19.

[156] See, e.g., AT&T Comments in re NBP PN # 4, filed Oct. 6, 2010, at 2.

[157] See, e.g., Rob Atkinson, President, Information Technology and Innovation Foundation Statement at the Broadband Accessibility for People with Disabilities II Workshop (Oct. 20, 2009).

[158] National Broadband Plan at 171-173.

[159] Id. at 174-178.

[160] Id.at 175.

[161] Id. at 178-181.

[162] Id. at 178.

[163] Id .at 178-179.

[164] Id. at 181.

[165] Id.

[166] Id. at 182.

[167] Id. at 181.

[168] Members of the BAWG would include representatives from the Departments of Agriculture, Commerce, Defense, Education, Health and Human Services, Justice, Labor, and Veterans' Administration; and the Access Board, the FCC, the Federal Trade Commission, the General Services Administration, the National Council on Disability, and the National Science Foundation. See id..

[169] National Broadband Plan at 181.

[170] Id.

[171] Id.

[172] Id.

[173] Id

[174] Id.

[175] Id.

[176] Id.

[177] Id.

[178] Id.

[179] Id.

[180] Id.

[181] See, e.g., Twenty-first Century Communications and Video Accessibility Act of 2009, H.R. 3101, 111th Cong. § 2 (2009) ("H.R. 3101"), introduced by Representative Markey. This recommendation is similar to a provision in H.R. 3101, § 717(d).

[182] National Broadband Plan at 182.

[183] Id.

[184] Id.

[185] Id.

[186] Id.

[187] Id.

[188] Id.

[189] Id. This recommendation is similar to a provision in H.R. 3101, § 102.

[190] 47 C.F.R. § 20.19(a).

[191] Amendment of the Commission's Rules Governing Hearing Aid-Compatible Mobile Handsets, WT Docket No. 07-250, Second Report and Order and Notice of Proposed Rulemaking, 22 FCC Rcd. 19670, 19702, para. 89 (2007) ("Wireless Hearing Aid Compatibility Notice").

[192] Wireless Hearing Aid Compatibility Notice, 22 FCC Rcd at 19704, para. 92.

[193] National Broadband Plan at 182.

[194] See Access Board Draft Guidelines at 80-82.

[195] This proceeding should be coordinated with the FCC proceeding addressing the future roles of 9-1-1 and NG9-1-1 as communications technologies, networks and architectures expand beyond traditional voice-centric devices.

[196] National Broadband Plan at 182. This recommendation is similar to a provision in H.R. 3101, § 201.

[197] National Broadband Plan at 182. In Motion Picture Ass'n of America, Inc. v. FCC, 309 F.3d 796 (D.C. Cir. 2002), the D.C. Circuit vacated the Commission's video description rules, finding that the Commission lacked the authority to adopt such rules.

[198] National Broadband Plan at 182.

[199] AT&T Comments in re NBP PN #4, filed Oct. 6, 2009, at 3 & 6.

[200] SMPTE Comments in re NBP PN #4, filed Oct. 6, 2009, at 2.

[201] ADA, § 302.

[202] National Broadband Plan at 182.

[203] Title II of the ADA requires that state and local governments make programs "readily accessible and usable" unless doing so would cause "fundamental alteration" to the structure or an "undue financial and administrative burden." ADA, § 506.

[204] See n. 115, supra.

[205] National Broadband Plan at 182.

[206] Id.

[207] Id.

[208] Id. This recommendation is similar to a provision in H.R. 3101, § 105(b)(2)(i)(1).

[209] See FCC Announces Agenda and Panelists for Workshop on VRS Reform To Be Held on December 17, 2009 Press Release (CBG Dec. 15, 2009), available at http://hraunfoss.fcc.gov/edocs_public/attachmatch/DOC-295208A1.doc

[210] National Broadband Plan at 182.

[211] See C. Marty Exline, Director, Missouri Assistive Technology Program Statement at Broadband Accessibility for People with Disabilities II Workshop (Oct. 20, 2009).

[212] Jim Tobias, Inclusive Technologies Statement at Workshop on Video Relay Service Reform (Dec. 17, 2009).

[213] National Broadband Plan at 182.

[214] See C. Marty Exline, Director, Missouri Assistive Technology Program Statement at Broadband Accessibility for People with Disabilities II Workshop (Oct. 20, 2009).

[215] See Rebecca Ladew, East Coast Representative, Speech Communications Assistance by Telephone, Inc. Statement at Broadband Accessibility for People with Disabilities II Workshop (Oct. 20, 2009) and Letter from Monica Martinez, Commissioner, Michigan Public Service Commission, to Julius Genachowski, Chairman, FCC,GN Docket Nos. 09-47, 09-51, 09-137; CS Docket No. 97-80 (Dec. 23, 2009) at 1.

[216] National Broadband Plan at 182.

[217] American Recovery and Reinvestment Act of 2009, Pub. L. No. 111-5, 123 Stat. 115, §6001 (k)(2) (2009).

[218] Department of Justice, International Treaty on the Rights of People with Disabilities, http://www.ada.gov/un_statement.htm (last visited Feb. 12, 2010). The Senate has not yet ratified the treaty.

[219] United Nations Enable, Convention on the Rights of Persons with Disabilities, Preamble (v), http://www.un.org/disabilities/default.asp?navid=13&pid=150. (last visited Feb. 12, 2010).

[220] American Association of People with Disabilities Comments in re NBP PN # 4, filed Oct. 6, 2010, at 2.

[221] 2005 Census Report at 4.

In: Emerging Technology Issues for People...   ISBN: 978-1-61122-523-5
Editors: Daniel B. Bernardino   © 2011 Nova Science Publishers, Inc.

Chapter 2

THE AMERICANS WITH DISABILITIES ACT: APPLICATION TO THE INTERNET

Nancy Lee Jones

SUMMARY

The Americans with Disabilities Act (ADA) provides broad nondiscrimination protection in employment, public services, public accommodations, and services operated by private entities, transportation, and telecommunications for individuals with disabilities. As stated in the act, its purpose is "to provide a clear and comprehensive national mandate for the elimination of

However, the ADA, enacted on July 26, 1990, prior to widespread use of the Internet, does not specifically cover the Internet, and the issue of coverage has not been definitively resolved. The Supreme Court has not addressed this issue, although there are some lower court decisions. The cases that directly discuss the ADA's application to the Internet vary in their conclusions about coverage.

INTRODUCTION

The Americans with Disabilities Act (ADA)[1] has often been described as the most sweeping nondiscrimination legislation since the Civil Rights Act of 1964. It provides broad nondiscrimination protection in employment, public services, public accommodations, and services operated by private entities, transportation, and telecommunications[2] for individuals with disabilities. As stated in the act, its purpose is "to provide a clear and comprehensive national mandate for the elimination of discrimination against individuals with disabilities."

However, the ADA, enacted on July 26, 1990, prior to widespread use of the Internet, does not specifically cover the Internet, and the issue of coverage has not been definitively resolved.[3] The Supreme Court has not addressed this issue, although there are some lower court decisions. Similarly, congressional action has been limited. The ADA was amended in 2008 to respond to a series of Supreme Court decisions that had interpreted the definition of disability narrowly but did not address the issue of Internet coverage.[4] On April 22, 2010, the Subcommittee on the Constitution, Civil Rights, and Civil Liberties of the House Judiciary Committee held a hearing on the ADA in the digital age.[5]

On July 26, 2010, the House passed H.R. 3101, 111th Congress, the Twenty-first Century Communications and Video Accessibility Act which, although it would not amend the ADA, in part requires Internet accessibility for individuals with disabilities.[6] A companion bill, S. 3304, 111th Congress, has been reported out of the Senate Committee on Commerce, Science, and Transportation.

The American Recovery and Reinvestment Act (ARRA)[7] did not specifically mention Internet accessibility, but did include the Health Information Technology for Economic and Clinical Health (HITECH) Act as part of P.L. 111-5,[8] and also directed the Federal Communications Commission (FCC) to develop a national broadband plan. The FCC released its plan on March 16, 2010.[9] One of the recommendations in this plan stated:

> The federal government should ensure the accessibility of digital content. The DOJ should amend its regulations to clarify the obligations of commercial establishments under Title III of the Americans with Disabilities Act with respect to commercial websites. The FCC should open a proceeding on the accessibility of video programming distributed over the Internet, the devices used to display such programming and related user interfaces, video

programming guides and menus. Congress should consider clarifying the FCC's authority to adopt video description rules.[10]

The ADA contains various requirements depending on whether the discrimination prohibited is in the employment context (Title I), is related to the activities of state or local governments (Title II), or concerns public accommodations (Title III). Although most of the judicial decisions and discussion of ADA applicability to the Internet have arisen regarding public accommodations, it is helpful to briefly examine employment and state and local government requirements.

EMPLOYMENT

Statutory Language

Title I of the ADA, as amended by the ADA Amendments Act of 2008, provides that no covered entity shall discriminate against a qualified individual on the basis of disability in regard to job application procedures; the hiring, advancement, or discharge of employees; employee compensation; job training; or other terms, conditions, and privileges of employment.[11] The term employer is defined as a person engaged in an industry affecting commerce who has 15 or more employees.[12] If the issue raised under the ADA is employment related, and the threshold issues of meeting the definition of an individual with a disability and involving an employer employing more than 15 individuals are met, the next step is to determine whether the individual is a qualified individual with a disability who, with or without reasonable accommodation, can perform the essential functions of the job.

Title I defines a "qualified individual with a disability." Such an individual is "an individual with a disability who, with or without reasonable accommodation, can perform the essential functions of the employment position that such person holds or desires."[13] The ADA requires the provision of reasonable accommodation unless the accommodation would pose an undue hardship on the operation of the business.[14]

"Reasonable accommodation" is defined in the ADA as including making existing facilities readily accessible to and usable by individuals with disabilities, job restructuring, part-time or modified work schedules, reassignment to a vacant position, acquisition or modification of equipment or devices, adjustment of examinations or training materials or policies, provision of qualified readers or interpreters, or other similar accommodations.[15] "Undue hardship" is defined as "an action requiring significant difficulty or expense."[16] Factors to be considered in determining whether an action would create an undue hardship include the nature and cost of the accommodation, the overall financial resources of the facility, the overall financial resources of the covered entity, and the type of operation or operations of the covered entity.

Judicial and Regulatory Interpretations

The ADA's statutory language specifically prohibits discrimination in "other terms, conditions, and privileges of employment."[17] The National Council on Disability (NCD)[18] has observed that "[n]o case or serious scholarly or legal argument has ever been found to support the proposition that because a job's functions involve electronic communication, employers are relieved of the obligation to consider reasonable accommodations or other measures aimed at facilitating equal access to the tools of the trade."[19] However, no judicial cases were found that specifically mandated website accessibility in the employment context. Despite this dearth of case law, it could be argued that Equal Employment Opportunity Commission (EEOC) policies on telework,[20] which is generally performed using computers, indicate that employment discrimination can encompass the lack of access to the Internet.[21]

STATE AND LOCAL GOVERNMENTS

Statutory Language

Title II of the ADA provides that no qualified individual with a disability shall be excluded from participation in or be denied the benefits of the services, programs, or activities of a public entity or be subjected to discrimination by any such entity.[22] "Public entity" is defined as state and local governments, any department or other instrumentality of a state or local government and certain transportation authorities. The ADA does not apply to the executive branch of the federal government; the executive branch and the

U.S. Postal Service are covered by Section 504 of the Rehabilitation Act of 1973.[23]

The Department of Justice (DOJ) regulations for Title II contain a specific section on program accessibility. Each service, program, or activity conducted by a public entity, when viewed in its entirety, must be readily accessible to and usable by individuals with disabilities. However, a public entity is not required to make each of its existing facilities accessible.[24] Program accessibility is limited in certain situations involving historic preservation. In addition, in meeting the program accessibility requirement, a public entity is not required to take any action that would result in a fundamental alteration in the nature of its service, program, or activity or in undue financial and administrative burdens.[25]

Judicial Interpretations

Like Title I, the case law and regulatory interpretations regarding the application of the ADA to the Internet are sparse under Title II.[26] However, one district court has examined accessibility issues regarding the website of a public transit system. In *Martin v. Metropolitan Atlanta Rapid Transit Authority,*[27] the court addressed a number of accessibility issues involving the Atlanta transit authority, including information accessibility. Noting that the information was available in several forms, including a website, the court found that the information was not equally accessible to individuals with disabilities even though some information was available by telephone. The court stated the following:

> MARTA representatives also concede that the system's web page is not formatted in such a way that it can be read by persons who are blind but who are capable of using text reader computer software for the visually impaired.... However, it now appears that MARTA is attempting to correct this problem. Until these deficiencies are corrected, MARTA is violating the ADA mandate of "making adequate communications capacity available, through accessible formats and technology, to enable users to obtain information and schedule service."[28]

Department of Justice and Department of Education Interpretations Regarding the Internet

In the April 2010 hearings before the House Judiciary Committee, Samuel R. Bagenstos, Principal Deputy Assistant Attorney General for Civil Rights at the Department of Justice, testified that "[t]here is no doubt that the Internet sites of State and local government entities are covered by Title II of the ADA."[29] He also noted that DOJ has published technical assistance, "Accessibility of State and Local Government Websites to People with Disabilities,"[30] which provides guidance for making government websites accessible.[31] Final regulations for Title II, issued on July 26, 2010, noted that "[t]he Department intends to engage in additional rulemaking in the near future addressing ... accessibility of websites operated by covered public entities and public accommodations."[32]

The concept of effective communications was also at issue in investigations by the Office of Civil Rights (OCR) at the Department of Education (ED). These OCR investigations involved access to various class and course related materials, including campus computer labs and the Internet, and generally resulted in required access.[33]

PUBLIC ACCOMMODATIONS

Statutory Provisions

Title III provides that no individual shall be discriminated against on the basis of disability in the full and equal enjoyment of the goods, services, facilities, privileges, advantages, or accommodations of any place of public accommodation by any person who owns, leases (or leases to), or operates a place of public accommodation.[34] Entities that are covered by the term "public accommodation" are listed, and include, among others, hotels, restaurants, theaters, auditoriums, laundromats, travel services, museums, parks, zoos, private schools, day care centers, professional offices of health care providers, and gymnasiums.[35] Religious institutions or entities controlled by religious institutions are not included on the list.

There are some limitations on the nondiscrimination requirements, and a failure to remove architectural barriers is not a violation unless such a removal is "readily achievable."[36] "Readily achievable" is defined as meaning "easily accomplishable and able to be carried out without much difficulty or expense."[37] Reasonable modifications in practices, policies, or procedures are required unless they would fundamentally alter the nature of the goods, services, facilities, or privileges or they would result in an undue burden.[38] An undue burden is defined as an action involving "significant difficulty or expense."[39]

Department of Justice Interpretations

Samuel R. Bagenstos, Principal Deputy Assistant Attorney General for Civil Rights at the Department of Justice, testified in the April 2010 hearings before the House Judiciary Committee that although case law has been limited, "the position of the Department of Justice has been clear: Title III applies to the Internet sites and services of private entities that meet the definition of public accommodations set forth in the statute and implementing regulations."[40] He also noted that DOJ is considering issuing guidance regarding the Internet sites of private businesses that are considered public accommodations under Title III of the ADA.[41] Mr. Bagenstos observed that the Department's position was first articulated in a response to a congressional inquiry. This response stated that "[c]overed entities that use the Internet for communications regarding their programs, goods, or services must be prepared to offer those communications through accessible means as well."[42] Final regulations for Title III, issued on July 26, 2010, noted that "[t]he Department intends to engage in additional rulemaking in the near future addressing ... accessibility of websites operated by covered public entities and public accommodations."[43]

DOJ has also argued that the ADA covers the Internet in amicus briefs.[44] In its report on the activities of the House Judiciary Committee following the hearings on the ADA and Internet accessibility on February 9, 2000, the House Judiciary Committee stated that "[i]t is the opinion of the Department of Justice that the ADA's accessibility requirements do apply to private Internet web sites and services."[45]

Place of Public Accommodation

As discussed previously, Title III prohibits discrimination in the full and equal enjoyment of the goods, services, facilities, privileges, advantages, or accommodations of any *place* of public accommodation by any person who owns, leases (or leases to), or operates a *place* of public accommodation.[46] One of the relevant issues in resolving the matter of whether Title III of the ADA applies to the Internet is whether a place of public accommodation is limited to actual physical structures.

Public Accommodations are not Limited to Physical Structures

The courts have split on this issue with the First Circuit in *Carparts Distribution Center v. Automotive Wholesalers Association of New England Inc.,*[47] finding that public accommodations are not limited to actual physical structures. The court reasoned that

> [b]y including "travel service" among the list of services considered "public accommodations," Congress clearly contemplated that "service establishments" include providers of services which do not require a person to physically enter an actual physical structure. Many travel services conduct business by telephone or correspondence without requiring their customers to enter an office in order to obtain their services. Likewise, one can easily imagine the existence of other service establishments conducting business by mail and phone without providing facilities for their customers to enter in order to utilize their services. It would be irrational to conclude that persons who enter an office to purchase services are protected by the ADA, but persons who purchase the same services over the telephone or by mail are not. Congress could not have intended such an absurd result.[48]

The First Circuit concluded that "to exclude this broad category of businesses from the reach of Title III and limit the application of Title III to physical structures which persons must enter to obtain goods and services would run afoul of the purposes of the ADA."[49]

The Seventh Circuit in *Doe v. Mutual of Omaha Insurance Company*[50] agreed with the First Circuit. In *Doe,* Judge Posner discussed the nondiscrimination requirements of Title III in the context of a case involving a cap on insurance policies for AIDS and AIDS-related complications and found that "[t]he core meaning of this provision, plainly enough, is that the owner or operator of a store, hotel, restaurant, dentist's office, travel agency, theater, website, or other facility (whether in physical space or in electronic space) ... that is open to the public cannot exclude disabled persons from entering the facility and, once in, from using the facility in the same way that the nondisabled do."[51] The court reasoned that "the owner or operator of, say, a camera store can neither bar the door to the disabled nor let them in but then refuse to sell its cameras to them on the same terms as to other customers."[52] However, Judge Posner found no violation of the ADA in this case and concluded that "Section 302(a) does not require a seller to alter his product to make it equally valuable to the disabled and nondisabled."[53]

The Second Circuit joined the First and Seventh Circuits in finding that the ADA is not limited to physical access. The court in *Pallozzi v. Allstate Life Insurance Co.,*[54] stated that "Title III's mandate that the disabled be accorded 'full and equal enjoyment of goods, [and] services ... of any place of public accommodation,' suggests to us that the statute was meant to guarantee them more than mere physical access."

Public Accommodations are Limited to Physical Structures

In contrast to the cases discussed above, the Third, Sixth, Ninth, and Eleventh Circuits apparently restrict the concept of public accommodations to physical places.

In *Stoutenbo rough v. National Football League, Inc.,*[55] the Sixth Circuit dealt with a case brought by an association of individuals with hearing impairments who filed suit against the National Football League (NFL) and several television stations under Title III alleging that the NFL's blackout rule discriminated against them since they had no other way of accessing football games when live telecasts are prohibited. The Sixth Circuit rejected this allegation holding that the prohibitions of Title III are restricted to places of public accommodations. Similarly, in *Parker v. Metropolitan Life Insurance Co.,*[56] the Sixth Circuit held that the ADA's nondiscrimination prohibition relating to public accommodations did not prohibit an employer from providing employees a disability plan that provided longer benefits for employees disabled by physical illness than those disabled by mental illness. In arriving at this holding, the Sixth Circuit found that "a benefit plan offered by an employer is not a good offered by a place of public accommodation.... A public accommodation is a physical place."[57]

In *Ford v. Schering-Plough Corp.*[58] and *Weyer v. Twentieth Century Fox Film Corp.,*[59] the Third and Ninth Circuits also found that a public accommodation must be a physical place. As the Third Circuit in *Ford* stated,

> [t]he plain meaning of Title III is that a public accommodation is a place.... This is in keeping with the host of examples of public accommodations provided by the ADA, all of which refer to places.... Since Ford received her disability benefits via her employment at Schering, she had

no nexus to MetLife's 'insurance office' and thus was not discriminated against in connection with a public accommodation.[60]

The Eleventh Circuit used similar reasoning in *Access Now, Inc. v. Southwest Airlines*, a case directly involved the ADA and the Internet.[61]

Judicial Decisions on Title III and the Internet

As noted above, the precise issue of the ADA's application to the Internet arose in *Access Now, Inc., v. Southwest Airlines, Co.*, where the district court held that the Southwest Airlines website was not a "place of public accommodation" and therefore was not covered by the ADA. The district court examined the ADA's statutory language, noting that all of the listed categories were concrete places, and that to expand the ADA to cover "virtual" spaces would be to create new rights.

Previously, on November 2, 1999, the National Federation of the Blind (NFB) filed a complaint against America Online (AOL) in federal district court alleging that AOL violated Title III of the ADA. NFB and other blind plaintiffs stated that they could only independently use computers by concurrently running screen access software programs for the blind that convert visual information into synthesized speech or braille. They alleged that AOL had designed its service so that it is incompatible with screen access software programs for the blind, failing "to remove communications barriers presented by its designs thus denying the blind independent access to this service, in violation of Title III of the ADA, 42 U.S.C. § 12181, et seq."[62] The case was settled on July 26, 2000.[63]

The most recent judicial decision on the ADA application to the Internet is *National Federation of the Blind v. Target Corporation*.[64] In *National Federation of the Blind,* the district court, taking a more nuanced approach, denied Target's motion to dismiss to the extent it alleged that the inaccessibility of the retailer's web site impeded the full and equal enjoyment of goods and services offered in the retailer's stores. The motion to dismiss was granted in part concerning the aspects of the website that offered information and services unconnected to the retailer's store. The court noted that the purpose of the ADA was "broader than mere physical access" and that "[t]o the extent defendant argues that plaintiffs' claims are not cognizable because they occur away from a 'place' of public accommodation, defendant's argument must fail." The court required that there be a "nexus" between the

Internet services and the physical place in order to present an actionable ADA claim.

The use of the "nexus" approach to the ADA's applicability to the Internet would cover many places of business such as Target. However, stores such as *Amazon.com* that have no physical storefront may not be covered under such an approach. The nexus approach has been criticized by the National Council of Disability:

> With the passage of time, as more and more goods, services, informational resources, recreation, communication, social and interactive activities of all kind migrate, wholly or partly, to the Net, maintenance of legal distinctions among otherwise similar Web sites, based on their connection or lack of connection to a physical facility, will become increasingly untenable and incoherent. Were there no nexus doctrine, and were all Web sites to be per se excluded from coverage, the law, however unjust, would at least be clear. But now that we see the direction in which the law, even in the hands of its most cautious interlocutors, is moving, the effort to define what is a sufficient nexus and to determine whether it exists in each particular case will surely continue. Use of the nexus approach, preferable as it may be to civil rights advocates over an approach that categorically excludes the Web from coverage, may, however, result in far more havoc than even the most sweeping and inclusive requirement for across-the-board commercial Web site accessibility ever could.[65]

CONCLUSION

The ADA was enacted in 1990, prior to widespread use of the Internet and does not specifically cover the Internet. Similarly, the ADA regulations do not specifically mention the Internet. However, the Department of Justice has indicated that it believes the ADA does require Internet accessibility. There has been no Supreme Court decision on point, and there have been few lower court judicial decisions. The lower courts that have examined the issue have split, creating some uncertainty. In addition, the use of a "nexus" approach in *National Federation of the Blind v. Target Corporation*, requiring a connection between the Internet services and the physical place in order to present an actionable ADA claim, would limit the application of the ADA to online retailers. Despite this uncertainty, it would appear likely that the Department of Justice's position would prevail, especially in light of the ADA's broad nondiscrimination mandate.

End Notes

[1] 42 U.S.C. § 12101 *et seq.* For a more detailed discussion of the ADA see CRS Report 98-921, *The Americans with Disabilities Act (ADA): Statutory Language and Recent Issues*, by Nancy Lee Jones.

[2] Title IV of the ADA amends Title II of the Communications Act of 1934 to ensure that individuals with hearing impairments are able to use telephones. 47 U.S.C. §225. One commentator has argued that Congress should use Title IV of the ADA as a model for adding an amendment specifically applying the ADA to the Internet. See Katherine Rengel, "The Americans with Disabilities Act and Internet Accessibility for the Blind," 25 John Marshall HJ. Computer & Info. L. 543 (2008).

[3] For a discussion of this issue see National Council on Disability (NCD), "The Need for Federal Legislation and Regulation Prohibiting Telecommunications and Information Services Discrimination," http://www.ncd.gov/ newsroom/publications/2006/pdf/discrimination.pdf. See also National Council on Disability (NCD), "National Disability Policy: A Progress Report" March 31, 2009, *http://www.ncd.gov/newsroom/publications/2009/pdf/* ProgressReport.pdf. It should be noted that federal government websites are required to be accessible under a separate statute, Section 508 of the Rehabilitation Act, 29 U.S.C. §794(d), as amended by P.L. 105-220. Section 508 requires that the electronic and information technology used by federal agencies be accessible to individuals with disabilities, including employees and members of the public. Generally, Section 508 requires each federal department or agency and the U.S. Postal Service to ensure that individuals with disabilities who are federal employees have access to and use of electronic and information technology that is comparable to that of individuals who do not have disabilities. For more detailed information see *http://www.section508.gov.*

[4] The ADA Amendments Act, P.L. 110-325. For a more detailed discussion of P.L. 110-325, see CRS Report RL34691, *The ADA Amendments Act: P.L. 110-325*, by Nancy Lee Jones.

[5] Achieving the Promise of the Americans with Disabilities Act in the Digital Age – Current Issues, Challenges, and Opportunities: Hearing Before the H. Subcommittee on the Constitution, Civil Rights, and Civil Liberties of the H. Comm. on the Judiciary, 110th Cong., 2d Sess. (2010), http://judiciary. Ten years earlier, hearings had also been held on the applicability of the ADA to private Internet sites, Applicability of the Americans with Disabilities Act (ADA) to Private Internet Sites: Hearing Before the H. Subcommittee on the Constitution of the H. Comm. on the Judiciary, 106th Cong. (2000).

[6] H.R. 3101 was reported out of the House Energy and Commerce Committee, H.Rept. 111-563. The Subcommittee on Communications, Technology and the Internet of the Senate Committee on Commerce, Science, and Transportation held a hearing on H.R. 3101, *Innovation and Inclusion: The Americans with Disabilities Act at 20: Hearing Before the S. Subcommittee on Communications, Technology and the Internet of the S. Comm. on Commerce, Science, and Transportation*, 110th Cong., 2d Sess. (2010), *http://commerce.senate.gov/public/index.cfm?p=Hearings&*ContentRecord_id=4c38a45b-a9f2-4458-a4d3-cb22c48714fd&ContentType_id=14f995b9-dfa5-407a-9d35-56cc7152a7ed&Group_id=b06c39af-e033-4cba-9221-de668ca1978a&MonthDisplay=5&YearDisplay=2010. This hearing focused on S. 3304, 1 10th Cong, Access to Communications in the 21st Century Act (Companion bill, H.R. 3104, 110th Cong.) which, in part, would require internet accessibility for individuals with disabilities but does not directly amend the ADA.

[7] P.L. 111-5.

[8] The HITECH Act is intended to promote the widespread adoption of health information technology (HIT) to support the electronic sharing of clinical data among hospitals, physicians, and other health care stakeholders. For a discussion of HITECH see CRS Report

R40161, *The Health Information Technology for Economic and Clinical Health (HITECH) Act*, by C. Stephen Redhead.

[9] FCC, "Connecting America: The National Broadband Plan," *http://www.broadband.gov/download-plan/*.

[10] *Id.* at p. 182.

[11] 42 U.S.C. §12112(a), as amended by P.L. 110-325, §5. The ADA Amendments Act strikes the prohibition of discrimination against a qualified individual with a disability because of the disability of such individual and substitutes the prohibition of discrimination against a qualified individual "on the basis of disability." The Senate Managers' Statement noted that this change "ensures that the emphasis in questions of disability discrimination is properly on the critical inquiry of whether a qualified person has been discriminated against on the basis of disability, and not unduly focused on the preliminary question of whether a particular person is a 'person with a disability.'" 153 CONG. REC. S8347 (Sept. 11, 2008)(Statement of Managers to Accompany S. 3406, the Americans with Disabilities Act Amendments Act of 2008).

[12] 42 U.S.C. §12111(5).

[13] 42 U.S.C. § 1211(8). The EEOC has stated that a function may be essential because (1) the position exists to perform the duty, (2) there are a limited number of employees available who could perform the function, or (3) the function is highly specialized. 29 C.F.R. §1630(n)(2).

[14] See 45 C.F.R. Part 84.

[15] 42 U.S.C. § 12111(9).

[16] 42 U.S.C. §12111(10).

[17] 42 U.S.C. §12112(a), as amended by P.L. 110-325, §5.

[18] NCD is an independent federal agency that provides advice to the President, Congress, and executive branch agencies to promote policies, programs, practices, and procedures that guarantee equal opportunity for all individuals with disabilities. See http://www.ncd.gov.

[19] National Council on Disability, "When the Americans with Disabilities Act Goes Online: Application of the ADA to the Internet and the Worldwide Web," (July 10, 2003) http://www.ncd.gov/newsroom/publications/2003/ adainternet.htm.

[20] EEOC, Fact Sheet: Work at Home: Telework as a Reasonable Accommodation (February 3, 2003), http://www.eeoc.gov/facts/telework.html.

[21] In addition, the National Federation of the Blind of Arkansas, the state of Arkansas, and the software provider SAP Public Services, Inc., entered into a settlement agreement in 2008 to resolve a suit by blind state employees who could not access the Arkansas administrative statewide information system. See http://www.NFB.org.

[22] 42 U.S.C. §§12131-12133.

[23] 29 U.S.C. §794.

[24] 28 C.F.R. §35.150.

[25] *Id.*

[26] For a discussion of how Titles II and III of the ADA might apply to internet access by students see Judith Stilz Ogden and Lawrence Menter, "Inaccessible School Webpages: Are Remedies Available?" 38 J. L. & Educ. 393 (2009).

[27] 225 F.Supp.2d 1362 (N.D. Ga. 2002).

[28] *Id.* at 1377. Quoting from the Department of Transportation ADA regulations, 49 C.F.R. §37.167(f).

[29] *Achieving the Promise of the Americans with Disabilities Act in the Digital Age – Current Issues, Challenges, and Opportunities: Hearing Before the H. Subcommittee on the Constitution, Civil Rights, and Civil Liberties of the H. Comm. on the Judiciary,* 110th Cong., 2d Sess. (2010), http://judiciary testimony of Samuel R. Bagenstos, Principal Deputy Assistant Attorney General for Civil Rights at the Department of Justice, http://judiciary.house.gov/hearings/pdf/Bagenstos100422.pdf.

[30] See http://www.usdoj.gov/crt/ada/websites2.htm.

[31] *Achieving the Promise of the Americans with Disabilities Act in the Digital Age – Current Issues, Challenges, and Opportunities: Hearing Before the H. Subcommittee on the Constitution, Civil Rights, and Civil Liberties of the H. Comm. on the Judiciary,* 110th Cong., 2d Sess. (2010), http://judiciary testimony of Samuel R. Bagenstos, Principal Deputy Assistant Attorney General for Civil Rights at the Department of Justice, http://judiciary.house.gov/hearings/pdf/Bagenstos100422.pdf.

[32] See http://www.ada.gov/regs2010/titleII_2010/reg2_2010.html.

[33] See http://people.rit.edu/easi/law.htm. For a more detailed discussion of this issue see National Council on Disability, "When the Americans with Disabilities Act Goes Online: Application of the ADA to the Internet and the Worldwide Web," (July 10, 2003) http://www.ncd.gov/newsroom/publications/2003/adainternet.htm.

[34] 42 U.S.C. §12182.

[35] 42 U.S.C. §12181.

[36] 42 U.S.C. §12182(b)(2)(A)(iv).

[37] 42 U.S.C. §12181.

[38] 42 U.S.C. §12182(b)(2)(A).

[39] 28 C.F.R. §36.104.

[40] Achieving the Promise of the Americans with Disabilities Act in the Digital Age – Current Issues, Challenges, and Opportunities: Hearing Before the H. Subcommittee on the Constitution, Civil Rights, and Civil Liberties of the H. Comm. on the Judiciary, 110th Cong., 2d Sess. (2010), http://judiciary testimony of Samuel R. Bagenstos, Principal Deputy Assistant Attorney General for Civil Rights at the Department of Justice, http://judiciary.house.gov/hearings/pdf/Bagenstos100422.pdf. In his testimony, Mr. Bagenstos also observed that accessibility issues arise in other technologies as well, and he specifically noted the increased use of electronic book readers by schools. DOJ and the Department of Education sent a joint letter to college and university presidents expressing concern about the use of inaccessible readers. See *http://www.ada.gov/*kindle_ ltr_ eddoj.htm. In addition, DOJ has resolved complaints against several universities concerning the use of inaccessible readers. See e.g., http://www.ada.gov/case_western_univ.htm; http://www.ada.gov/reed_college.htm; http://www.ada.gov/pace_univ.htm; *http://www*. ada. gov/ princeton.htm.

[41] *Id.*

[42] Letter from Deval L. Patrick, Assistant Attorney General, Civil Rights Division, to Tom Harkin, U.S. Senator (September 9, 1996) http://www.usdoj.gov/crt/foia/tal712.txt One commentator has argued that this letter is limited in its scope since it applies its requirements only to "covered entities" which the letter defined as state and local governments and places of public accommodation. See Katherine Rengel, "The Americans with Disabilities Act and Internet Accessibility for the Blind," 25 John Marshal J. of Computer & Information Law 543 (2008).

[43] See http://www.ada.gov/regs2010/titleIII_2010/reg3_2010.html.

[44] See e.g., Amicus Brief of the United States filed in the Fifth Circuit in Hooks v. OKBridge, Inc. (No 99-50891) "The language of the statute is broad enough to cover services provided over this new medium and courts are not reluctant to apply old words to new technology in a way that is consistent with modern usage and legislative intent." http://www.usdoj.gov/ crt/briefs/hooks.htm.

[45] H.Rept. 106-1048, at 275 (2001). One commentator has argued that this statement, combined with the lack of congressional action, indicates that Congress is "deferring to the DOJ's authority to promulgate rules implementing Title III instead of amending Title III or drafting new legislation." Ali Abrar and Kerry J. Dingle, "From Madness to Method: the Americans with Disabilities Act Meets the Internet" 44 Harv. C.R.-C.L. L. Rev. 133, 155 (2009).

[46] 42 U.S.C. §12182 (emphasis added).

[47] *Carparts Distribution Center, Inc. v. Automotive Wholesalers' Association of New England, Inc.,* 37 F.3d 12 (1st Cir. 1994).

[48] *Id.* at 22.

[49] *Id.* at 26-27.

[50] 179 F.3d 557 (7th Cir. 1999), *cert. denied,* 528 U.S. 1106 (2000).

[51] *Id.* at 559 (emphasis added.)

[52] *Id.*

[53] *Id.* at 563.

[54] 198 F.3d 28 (2d Cir. 1999).

[55] 59 F.3d 580 (6th Cir. 1995), *cert. denied,* 516 U.S. 1028 (1995).

[56] 121 F.3d 1006 (6th Cir. 1997), *cert. denied,* 522 U.S. 1084 (1998).

[57] *Id.* At 1010. See also, *Lenox v. Healthwise of Kentucky,* 149 F.3d 453 (6th Cir. 1999).

[58] 145 F.3d 601 (3rd Cir. 1998).

[59] 198 F.3d 1104 (9th Cir. 2000).

[60] 145 F.3d 601, 613 (3rd Cir. 1998).

[61] 227 F.Supp.2d 1312 (S.D. Fla. 2002), appeal dismissed on other grounds, 385 F.3d 1324 (1 1th Cir. 2004). But see Rendon v. Valleycrest Productions, 294 F.3rd 1279 (1 1th Cir. 2002), where the Eleventh Circuit found a violation of the ADA in the use of telephone selection process that tended to screen out individuals with disabilities.

[62] *National Federation of the Blind v. America Online,* Complaint, *http://www.nfb.org/Images/nfb/Publications/bm/*bm99/brlm9912.htm (November 2, 1999).

[63] The settlement agreement can be found at the National Federation of the Blind website, http://www.nfb.org.

[64] 452 F.Supp.2d 946 (N.D. Calif. 2006). The case was settled on August 27, 2008. See http://www.nfb.org. For a more detailed discussion of this case see Isabel Arana DuPree, "Websites as 'Places of Public Accommodation': Amending the Americans with Disabilities Act in the Wake of *National Federal of the Blind v. Target Corporation,*" NC J. L. & Tech. 273 (2007); Jeffrey Bashaw, "Applying the Americans with Disabilities Act to Private Websites after *National Federation of the Blind v. Target,*" 4 Shidler J. L. Com. & Tech. 3 (2008).

[65] National Council on Disability, "When the Americans with Disabilities Act Goes Online: Application of the ADA to the Internet and the Worldwide Web," (July 10, 2003) http://www.ncd.gov/newsroom/publications/2003/adainternet.htm. See also Nikki D. Kessling, "Why the Target 'Nexus Test' Leaves Disabled Americans Disconnected: A Better Approach to Determine Whether Private Commercial Websites are 'Places of Public Accommodations,'" 45 Houston L. Rev. 991 (2008) where the author argued that the nexus test does not reflect statutory intent and that ADA coverage of a website should depend on the website's "commerciality and character;" Ali Abrar and Kerry J. Dingle, "From Madness to Method: The Americans with Disabilities Act Meets the Internet," 44 Harv. C.R.-C.L. L. Rev. 133 (2009), where is it argued that the nexus test is both under and over inclusive.

In: Emerging Technology Issues for People...   ISBN: 978-1-61122-523-5
Editors: Daniel B. Bernardino   © 2011 Nova Science Publishers, Inc.

Chapter 3

STATEMENT OF SAMUEL R. BAGENSTOS, PRINCIPAL DEPUTY ASSISTANT ATTORNEY GENERAL FOR CIVIL RIGHTS, DEPARTMENT OF JUSTICE, BEFORE THE SUBCOMMITTEE ON THE CONSTITUTION, CIVIL RIGHTS AND CIVIL LIBERTIES, HEARING ON "EMERGING TECHNOLOGIES AND THE RIGHTS OF INDIVIDUALS WITH DISABILITIES"

Chairman Nadler, Ranking Member Sensenbrenner, and Members of the Subcommittee, it is an honor to appear before you today to discuss the rights of individuals with disabilities to have access to emerging technologies. The Civil Rights Division enforces the Americans with Disabilities Act ("ADA") and Section 504 of the Rehabilitation Act, and we have a substantial role in implementing Section 508 of the Rehabilitation Act. Pursuant to these statutes, access to the internet and emerging technologies is not simply a technical matter, but a fundamental issue of civil rights. As more and more of our social infrastructure is made available on the internet – in some cases, exclusively online B access to information and electronic technologies is increasingly becoming the gateway civil rights issue for individuals with disabilities.

Congress adopted the Americans with Disabilities Act in 1990. The statute is a comprehensive, broad-reaching mandate to eliminate discrimination on the basis of disability in all of the areas of American civic and economic life. The Department of Justice is responsible for enforcement and implementation of Titles II and III of the ADA, which cover State and local government entities and private businesses, respectively. We also enforce Title I of the ADA, which prohibits disability discrimination in employment, in cases involving State and local government employees. Most of the nondiscrimination requirements of Title III apply to private businesses that fall within one of the categories of "public accommodation" established in the statute and the Attorney General's implementing regulations. The Department also enforces the statute on which the ADA is based, Section 504 of the Rehabilitation Act of 1973, 29 U.S.C. 794, which prohibits discrimination in federally assisted and federally conducted programs and activities.

When Congress enacted the ADA and Section 504, the internet as we know it today – the ubiquitous venue for information, commerce, services, and activities – did not exist. For that reason, although the ADA and Section 504 guarantee the protection of the rights of individuals with disabilities in a broad array of activities, neither law expressly mentions the internet or contains requirements regarding developing technologies. When Congress amended the Rehabilitation Act in 1998, it added section 508. That provision specifically requires Federal government agencies to ensure that their electronic and information technologies, including their websites, are accessible to individuals with disabilities. 29 U.S.C. 794(d). Within the Civil Rights Division the Disability Rights Section is responsible for enforcement of the civil rights statutes relating to the accessibility of information technologies to individuals with disabilities.

In this testimony, I will first discuss the importance of accessible technology to people with disabilities. I will then talk about the significant barriers that keep people with disabilities from having full and equal access to emerging technologies. I will then discuss the actions the Department of Justice is taking to ensure that emerging technologies do not leave people with disabilities behind.

DISABILITY RIGHTS AND DEVELOPING TECHNOLOGIES

Information technologies play a significant and ever expanding role in everyday life in America. The most developed and entrenched of these technologies, the internet, has become a gateway to the full range of activities, goods, and services available offline. Constituents of State and local government use the internet to renew library books and driver's licenses, to file tax forms, and even to correspond with elected officials. Increasingly, businesses – even those with substantial physical sales facilities – use websites to sell goods and services to their customers. So-called e-commerce is a rapidly expanding segment of the American economy. Ensuring nondiscriminatory access to the goods and services offered through the internet is therefore essential to full societal participation by individuals with disabilities.

It is not simply e-commerce that is affected, however. Electronic and information technologies are swiftly becoming a gateway to employment and education. Employment recruiting and hiring systems are often web based. In many cases, the only way to apply for a job or to sign up for an interview is on the internet. Job applicants research employment opportunities online, and they use the internet to most efficiently learn about potential employers' needs and policies. And schools at all levels are increasingly offering programs and classroom instruction through the internet. Many colleges and universities offer degree programs online; some universities exist exclusively on the internet. Even if they do not offer degree programs online, most colleges and universities today rely upon the internet and other electronic and information technologies in course assignments and discussion groups, and for a wide variety of administrative and logistical functions in which students and staff must participate.

For many individuals with disabilities who are limited in their ability to travel or who are confined to their homes, the internet is one of the few available means of access to the goods and services of our society. The broad mandate of the ADA to provide an equal opportunity for individuals with disabilities to participate in and benefit from all aspects of American civic and economic life will be served in today's technologically advanced society only if it is clear to businesses, employers, and educators, among others, that their web sites must be accessible.

But the internet is not the only information or electronic technology that is altering the way in which we do business and provide education in this country. Facing an exponential rise in the cost of standard print text books, colleges and universities are beginning to use electronic books and electronic book readers instead. Electronic book readers are typically lightweight, hand-held devices with screens and operating controls. Texts in an electronic form appear on the screens of these devices to simulate the experience of reading a book. The texts that appear on screen are formatted to look just like they would in a print version. Colleges and universities are likely to use digital and electronic text books more and more. Some experts predict that traditional print texts will be replaced by electronic or digital texts within three to five years.

As public servants entrusted with the welfare of our citizens, we in the Federal government must provide the leadership to make certain that individuals with disabilities are not excluded from the virtual world in the same way that they were historically excluded from "brick and mortar" facilities. Emerging technology promises to open up opportunities for people with disabilities throughout our society. But a digital divide is growing between individuals with and without disabilities. If we are not careful, as technology becomes more sophisticated the gap will grow wider, and people with disabilities will have less access to our public life.

These problems—and the corresponding opportunities—are likely to become more acute in the years to come. As the population ages, more and more Americans will need access to emerging technologies to continue working and to access the healthcare system. The 2006 National Health Interview Survey (NHIS), revealed that 13.6 percent of Americans 65 to 74 years of age reported having a vision loss and 21.7 percent of Americans 75 years of age and older reported having a vision loss. Advances in the availability of accessible technologies will increase—and are already increasing—the long-term employability of individuals with progressive blindness and other vision disabilities.

TECHNOLOGICAL BARRIERS TO ACCESSIBILITY

Millions of people have disabilities that affect their use of the web – including people with visual, auditory, physical, speech, cognitive, and neurological disabilities. People who are blind or have low vision are often the most affected by inaccessible information and electronic technology.[1] Many individuals with visual impairments use an assistive technology known as a screen reader that enables them to access the information on computers or internet sites. Screen readers read text aloud as it appears on the computer screen. Individuals who are blind may also use refreshable Braille displays, which convert the text of websites to Braille. Sometimes, those individuals will use keyboards in lieu of a mouse to move up and down on a screen or sort through a list and select an item.

The most common barriers on websites are posed by images or photographs that do not provide identifying text. A screen reader or similar assistive technology cannot "read" an image. When images appear on websites without identifying text, therefore, there is no way for the individual who is blind or who has low vision to know what is on the screen. The simple addition of a tag or other description of the image or picture will keep an individual using a screen reader oriented and allow him or her to gain access to the information the image depicts. Similarly, complex websites often lack navigational headings or links that would make them easy to navigate using a screen reader. Web designers can easily add those headings. They may also add cues to ensure the proper functioning of keyboard commands. They can also set up their programs to respond to voice interface technology. Making websites accessible is neither difficult nor especially costly, and in most cases providing accessibility will not result in changes to the format or appearance of a site.

Accessibility issues arise outside of the internet as well. Most significantly, as schools increasingly use electronic texts, the inaccessibility of many electronic book readers has become more and more salient. At the same time, however, the use of electronic texts holds great promise for people with disabilities. Students who are blind or have low vision have long used a form of electronic text as an accommodation that enables them to access the course materials their classmates use. These electronic texts, which are converted from standard print texts, are read on a computer, using a screen reader or a refreshable Braille display. In order for these electronic texts to be truly usable by someone who is blind or who has low vision, however, the texts must be coded with structural data so that the assistive technology can properly identify where to begin reading or where a sentence or paragraph begins and ends.

This system disadvantages blind students in colleges and universities as compared with sighted students, because it can take considerable time for a university to locate texts from publishers, and convert the text to a format usable by a screen reader or similar assistive technology. As a result, all too often course materials are not available to blind students until well after classes have begun.[2] If you ask just about any disability student services center at a major university, you will learn how significant this problem really is. Imagine as a student being unable – on a routine basis – to obtain your course materials for the first four months of the semester. As an alternative to obtaining converted texts from the publisher, universities may scan printed texts in order to provide them in electronic form. But this method can result in a "text dump," which lacks structural data to ensure proper reading by assistive technologies. Conversion errors, too, are common. So, the choice available to blind students prior to use of the new, electronic book readers, was to receive accurate materials months into the semester or inaccurate materials in a more timely manner.

The emergence of dedicated electronic book readers thus holds great potential to place students with disabilities on equal footing with other students. But that happy result will occur only if the electronic book reader is equipped with text-to-speech capabilities, so that it may read the electronic text aloud. In a few moments, I will discuss the Department of Justice's settlements in investigations of colleges and universities that used the Kindle DX, an inaccessible electronic book reader, as part of a pilot project. At the time the Kindle DX was used in this pilot project, it contained text-to-speech capabilities – meaning that it could read the electronic text aloud, rendering the text audible and therefore accessible to blind persons. Unfortunately, the device did not include a similar audio option for the menus or navigational controls. Without text-to-speech for the menu or navigational controls, blind students could not operate the electronic book reader independently, because they had no way of knowing which book they selected or how to access the search, note taking, or bookmark functions of the device. Electronic book readers developed by companies other than Amazon also pose barriers to use by individuals who are blind or have low vision, typically because they entirely lack a text-to-speech function.

But a dedicated electronic book reader can be made accessible. From the user perspective, an accessible electronic book reader might speak each option on a menu aloud, as the cursor moves over it, and then speak the selected choice aloud once made by the user. Special key strokes might be programmed specifically for blind users. For example, the user would press the alt-A key any time something related to accessibility is needed, at which point a menu with additional choices would come up allowing the user to scroll over the menu as described above. Appropriate coding would mean that the text, even mathematical formulas, or poetry in which line lengths vary, would be read aloud coherently. In this way, the user with the disability would gain access to all the information on the printed page.

THE DEPARTMENT OF JUSTICE POSITIONS REGARDING WEBSITE ACCESSIBILITY

Ensuring that people with disabilities have a full and equal opportunity to access the benefits of emerging technologies is an essential part of our disability rights enforcement at the Department of Justice. Because the internet was not in general public use when Congress enacted the ADA and the Attorney General promulgated regulations to implement it, neither the statute nor the regulations expressly mention it. But the statute and regulations create general rules designed to guarantee people with disabilities equal access to all of the important areas of American civic and economic life. And the Department made clear, in the preamble to the original 1992 ADA regulations, that the regulations should be interpreted to keep pace with developing technologies. 28 C.F.R. pt. 36, App. B.

The Department of Justice has long taken the position that both State and local government websites *and* the websites of private entities that are public accommodations are covered by the ADA. In other words, the websites of entities covered by both Title II and Title III of the statute are required by law to ensure that their sites are fully accessible to individuals with disabilities. The Department is considering issuing guidance on the range of issues that arise with regard to the internet sites of private businesses that are public accommodations covered by Title III of the ADA. In so doing, the Department will solicit public comment from the broad range of parties interested in this issue.

There is no doubt that the internet sites of State and local government entities are covered by Title II of the ADA. Similarly, there is no doubt that the websites of recipients of Federal financial assistance are covered by Section 504 of the Rehabilitation Act. The Department of Justice has affirmed the application of these statutes to internet sites in a technical assistance publication, *Accessibility of State and Local Government Websites to People with Disabilities* (http://www.usdoj.gov/crt/ada/websites2.htm), and in numerous agreements with State and local governments and recipients of Federal financial assistance. Our technical assistance publication also provides guidance with simple steps to ensure that government websites have accessible features for individuals with disabilities.

As to private places of public accommodation, only two cases – both in Federal district courts – have specifically addressed the application of ADA Title III to their websites, and those cases have reached different conclusions.

But the position of the Department of Justice has been clear: Title III applies to the internet sites and services of private entities that meet the definition of "public accommodations" set forth in the statute and implementing regulations. The Department first made this position public in a 1996 letter from Assistant Attorney General Deval Patrick responding to an inquiry by Senator Harkin regarding the accessibility of websites to individuals with visual impairments. The letter has been widely cited as illustration of the Department's position. The letter does not state whether entities doing business exclusively on the internet are covered by the ADA. In 2000, however, the Department filed an amicus brief in the Fifth Circuit in *Hooks v. OKbridge*, which involved a web-only business; the Department's brief explained that a business providing services solely over the internet is subject to the ADA's prohibitions on discrimination on the basis of disability.[3] And in a 2002 amicus brief in the Eleventh Circuit in *Rendon v. Valleycrest Productions*, the Department argued against a requirement, imposed outside of the internet context by some Federal courts of appeals, that there be a nexus between the challenged activity and a private entity's brick-and-mortar facility to obtain coverage under Title III. Although *Rendon* did not involve the internet, our brief argued that Title III applies to any activity or service offered by a public accommodation either on or off the premises.[4]

The Disability Rights Section of the Department of Justice's Civil Rights Division began to provide technical assistance to a host of public and private entities that were in the process of assisting Federal agencies with Section 508 compliance, and much of its guidance on making internet sites accessible developed from there. There are several sets of standards describing how to make websites accessible to individuals with disabilities. Government standards for website accessibility were developed pursuant to Section 508. Many entities elect to use the standards that were developed and are maintained by the Web Accessibility Initiative, a subgroup of the World Wide Web Consortium ("W3C®").

THE DEPARTMENT OF JUSTICE POSITIONS REGARDING OTHER EMERGING TECHNOLOGIES

In June of last year, the Department of Justice received several complaints from the National Federation of the Blind ("NFB"), the American Council of the Blind ("ACB"), and a coalition of disability rights groups collectively known as the Reading Rights Coalition – each alleging that colleges or universities were violating their obligations under the ADA and Section 504 by having their students use electronic book readers that were inaccessible to individuals who are blind for course materials. Case Western Reserve University, Princeton University, Pace University, Reed College, and Arizona State University, among others, had formed a pilot project with Amazon.com, Inc., to evaluate the viability of using the Kindle DX in a classroom setting. The NFB and the ACB, along with an individual blind plaintiff, also filed suit in Federal district court against Arizona State University; they argued that the pilot project violated Title II and Section 504. *Nat'l Fed. of the Blind , et al. v. Arizona Bd. of Regents, et al.*, Case No. CV 09-1359 GMS (D. Az. 2009).

The Department of Justice investigated each complaint and, on January 13, 2010, the Department issued a press release announcing that it had reached separate settlement agreements with Case Western Reserve University, Reed College, and Pace University.[5] The Department of Justice and the NFB and the ACB also jointly settled the litigation against Arizona State University in an agreement signed on January 11, 2010. Since that time, on March 29, 2010, the Department entered into a final settlement agreement with Princeton University.

These settlement agreements provide that the universities will not purchase, require, or in any way incorporate into the curriculum the Kindle DX or any other dedicated electronic book reader that is not fully accessible to individuals who are blind or have low vision. The agreements become effective at the end of the pilot projects. The agreements also contain a functional definition of accessibility when applied to dedicated electronic book readers – the universities must ensure that students who are blind or have low vision are able to access and acquire the same information, engage in the same interactions, and enjoy the same services as sighted students with substantially equivalent ease of use. The purpose behind these agreements is to underscore that requiring use of an emerging technology in the classroom that is inaccessible to an entire population of individuals with disabilities–individuals with visual disabilities–is discrimination that is prohibited by the Americans with Disabilities Act of 1990 ("ADA") and Section 504 of the Rehabilitation Act of 1973 ("Section 504").

During the course of its investigations and negotiations with the colleges and universities, Amazon.com, Inc., which is not covered by the ADA or Section 504 in its capacity as the manufacturer of the Kindle DX, posted a notice on its website indicating its intention to make the menu and navigational controls of the Kindle DX fully accessible to individuals who are blind or have low vision by extending the text-to-speech feature to these functions by the end of the year 2010.

The accessibility of electronic text readers stands to improve dramatically the experience of students with visual disabilities. The instantaneous downloading of texts is obviously a "night and day" difference for blind students who are used to waiting for their materials until well into the semester or to receiving inferior materials that are difficult to follow. Moreover, if accessible electronic book readers are used in the classrooms of the future, students with and without disabilities will be able to use the same devices, albeit in different ways, resulting in an integrated experience for students with disabilities who will not have to rely on separate accommodations to gain access to course materials. Such integration is the core goal of the ADA and Section 504.

As we come to realize anew each day, the pace of technological change is amazing; what appeared impossible just months or years ago is now commonplace. Advancing technology can open doors for people with disabilities and provide the means for them to have full, equal, and integrated access to American life. But technological advances will leave people with disabilities behind if technology developers and manufacturers do not make their new products accessible. In carrying out its responsibilities under the ADA and the Rehabilitation Act, the Federal government must make sure that the legal protections for the rights of individuals with disabilities are clear and sufficiently strong to ensure that innovation increases opportunities for everyone. We must avoid the travesty that would occur if the doors that are opening to Americans from advancing technologies were closed for individuals with disabilities because we were not vigilant.

I look forward to answering any questions that Members of the Subcommittee may have.

End Notes

[1] People who have difficulty using a computer mouse because of mobility impairments, for example, may use an assistive technology that allows them to control software with verbal commands. But websites and other technologies are not always compatible with those assistive technologies. Captioning of streaming videos may also be necessary in order to make them accessible to individuals who are deaf or hard of hearing. And individuals with difficult memory or cognitive impairments may be affected by complex websites.

[2] As the Disability Resource Center ("Center") at Arizona State University, one of the universities involved in the Kindle matter that I will discuss in a moment, informs blind students in its handbook, for example, "textbook/print conversion is a time intensive

process, especially for technical subject matter, and *can require up to four months to complete." See www.asu.edu/* studentaffairs/ed/drc/ services_alternative_format _procedure. htm. (emphasis added).

[3] *Department of Justice Brief as Amicus Curiae* at p. 7, Case No. SA-99-CV-214-EP, Aug. 1, 2000 (on appeal from the United States District Court for the Western District of Texas.) The unpublished, per curiam opinion can be found at 232 F.3d 208 (5th Cir. 2000).

[4] *Department of Justice Brief as Amicus Curiae,* Case No. 01-11197, June 18, 2002 (on appeal from the United States District Court of the Southern District of Florida). 294 F.3d 1279 (11th Cir. 2002).

[5] Agreement between United States and Case Western Reserve University, Jan. 13, 2010; Agreement between United States and Pace University, Jan. 13, 2010; Agreement between United States and Reed College, Jan. 13, 2010.

In: Emerging Technology Issues for People…   ISBN: 978-1-61122-523-5
Editors: Daniel B. Bernardino   © 2011 Nova Science Publishers, Inc.

Chapter 4

STATEMENT OF THE AMERICAN FOUNDATION FOR THE BLIND, (PREPARED BY MARK D. RICHERT, ESQ.), BEFORE THE SUBCOMMITTEE ON THE CONSTITUTION, CIVIL RIGHTS AND CIVIL LIBERTIES, HEARING ON "ACHIEVING THE PROMISE OF THE AMERICANS WITH DISABILITIES ACT IN THE DIGITAL AGE-CURRENT ISSUES, CHALLENGES AND OPPORTUNITIES"

INTRODUCTION

Good afternoon, Chairman Nadler and Subcommittee members, and thank you for the opportunity to share with you our enthusiasm for the work that the U.S. Department of Justice is undertaking to make it clear that the Americans with Disabilities Act (ADA) will continue to be the emancipation proclamation for all people with disabilities in the digital age. Indeed, the title of today's hearing, *Achieving the Promise of the ADA*, could easily be reworded to *Keeping the Promise of the ADA*. People with disabilities have always been confident in our understanding that the reach and relevance of the ADA can, does, and must endure in a world that is increasingly reliant on technology and the Internet in literally every area of daily life.

My name is Mark Richert, and I serve as the Public Policy Director for the American Foundation for the Blind (AFB), the national organization to which Helen Keller devoted more than four decades of her extraordinary life. I am proud to speak this afternoon on behalf of the more than 25 million Americans living with significant vision loss. In addition I serve as a co-chair of the Civil Rights Task Force of the 100-organization-member Consortium for Citizens with Disabilities and a co-founder of the Coalition of Organizations for Accessible Technology, the nation's largest cross-disability coalition advocating for the right of all people with disabilities to full access to telecommunications and video technologies. I am keenly aware of the power of technology and the Internet to transform the lives of tens of millions of Americans living with a variety of disabilities. I also know from personal experience that, in many instances, unusable Internet sites and inaccessible communications and high-speed data equipment serve as the very barriers to employment, civic participation and quality of life that such powerful tools can and should be particularly useful in breaking down. Following the charge of today's hearing to explore the major issues, challenges and opportunities about which we must be aware to fully realize the promise of the ADA in the digital age, let me first turn to a very brief analysis of the public policy context in which we are having this discussion.

ISSUES

Although no one could have fully grasped in 1990 when the ADA was enacted exactly how technology would so fundamentally transfigure our lives, all who gloried in the ADA becoming the law of the land rallied behind one overarching moral call, as the first President Bush proclaimed it, to "Let the *shameful wall* of exclusion finally come tumbling down." Internet inaccessibility is itself a shameful and unnecessary obstacle but with the added complication of being somewhat less visible than the physical steps that even today may bar people with disabilities from entering a place of employment, a store or courthouse. When access to employment, education and information is locked behind an inaccessible website, access to justice and full participation in society is denied for people with disabilities. This is why the disability community has long understood that the ADA is as essential in the digital age as it has always been.

The question is not whether the ADA applies to the Internet. Rather, the ADA applies, as it has always applied, to a range of entities who are not and should not be free to shut out people with disabilities virtually just as they may not do so physically. An array of divergent court decisions have scrambled the common sense understanding that the ADA's nondiscrimination mandate applies to public accommodations regardless of the modality they use to conduct business, in person, by phone or online. As a result, the disability community has consistently called for the U.S. Department of Justice (DOJ) to bring some order out of this needless chaos and restate, with specificity, the ADA's role in ensuring accessible e-commerce.

As the Presidentially-appointed National Council on Disability (NCD) declared in its 2009 ADA Progress Report (*www.ncd.gov/newsroom/* publications/2009/publications.htm):

> Use of the Internet is an inherent part of life today. For people with disabilities, however, access is not guaranteed. Because the ADA was passed before the Internet became pervasive, and the Department of Justice (DOJ) regulations do not address Internet access specifically, many Web sites still are not designed to be accessible by people with certain disabilities. ... Implementation of the Section 508 Web Accessibility standards in the Federal sector, as well as the global impact of the World Wide Web Consortium's Web accessibility standards, demonstrate that the means for making Web sites accessible are well-established, and a Federal requirement for full accessibility of public Web sites is long overdue.

In 2003, NCD released "Application of the ADA to the Internet and the Worldwide Web"(*www.ncd.gov/newsroom/publications/2003/*publications. htm) in which the issues and case law surrounding Internet access were examined. Concluding that public accommodations are not relieved of their nondiscrimination obligations under the ADA merely by moving online, the NCD called on DOJ to clarify the rights of people with disabilities to have access to the Internet. Since that time, people with disabilities have had to continue to fight for access to commercial web sites, including having to resort to litigation.

Most recently, the Federal Communications Commission (FCC) released its much-anticipated *National Broadband Plan*, a comprehensive set of policy objectives intended to make broadband affordable and accessible to all Americans. Among its many significant recommendations of particular impact on the lives of people with disabilities, the FCC is calling for the following:

Accessibility laws, regulations and subsidy programs should be updated to cover Internet Protocol (IP)-based communications and video-programming technologies. To do so: The FCC should ensure services and equipment are accessible to people with disabilities. The FCC should extend its Section 255 rules to require providers of advanced services and manufacturers of end-user equipment, network equipment and software used for advanced services to make their products accessible to people with disabilities. ...The federal government should ensure the accessibility of digital content. The DOJ should amend its regulations to clarify the obligations of commercial establishments under Title III of the Americans with Disabilities Act with respect to commercial websites. The FCC should open a proceeding on the accessibility of video programming distributed over the Internet, the devices used to display such programming and related user interfaces, video programming guides and menus.

In addition to the FCC's recommendation that DOJ's ADA regulations be clarified to resolve any lingering doubts about the relevance of the ADA to commercial websites, the FCC is recognizing in its recommendations the inextricable connection today between use of the Internet itself and the accessibility of the devices and services needed to access the Internet. This is why, though the anticipated improvements to the ADA rules announced by DOJ are critical, such a move is only one vital piece of the policy puzzle. As people with disabilities, the sites we visit online that are run by employers, governments and public accommodations that the ADA covers must be accessible to us, but the mobile and other technologies we use to get there must themselves be accessible.

CHALLENGES

Research reveals that Internet use by people with disabilities is much lower than that of the general population. Specifically, fewer than 30% of people with disabilities over the age of 15 were shown to have access to the Internet, compared to more than 60% of people without disabilities. Also, people with disabilities in both metropolitan and non-metropolitan areas have lower rates of Internet use than their geographic counterparts with no disability, with non-metropolitan people with disabilities having the lowest rate of Internet use (26.7%) of all groups. (See Enders, Alexandra. "Ruralfacts: Disability and the Digital Divide: Comparing Surveys with Disability Data." Research and Training Center on Disability in Rural Communities, The

University of Montana Rural Institute, Missoula, MT. June 2006, at http://rtc.ruralinstitute.umt.edu/TelCom/Divide.htm; *See also* Dobransky, Kerry and Hargittai, Eszter. "The Disability Divide in Internet Access and Use." *Information, Communication and Society.* 9(3):313-334. June 2006 at http://eszter.com/research/a18-disabilitydivide.html.)

Moreover, this past February, the FCC released the results of a consumer survey (conducted in October 2009), *Broadband Adoption & Use in America*, that found affordability and lack of digital skills are the main reasons why 93 million people -- or one third of the country -- are not connected to high speed Internet at home. Perhaps most astoundingly the survey found that 39 percent of all Americans without broadband have some type of disability. (See FCC's "Broadband Adoption & Use in America," at *http://hraunfoss.fcc.gov/edocs_public/attachmatch/DOC-296442A1.pdf*.)

These numbers demonstrate, among other things, that people with disabilities are being left behind as America migrates to broadband. There are of course many factors contributing to this inequity, particularly the inability of many people with disabilities to afford high-speed connection to the Internet. These challenges, however, are further exacerbated by the routine every-day experience of people with disabilities who, once they get online, run into very real barriers.

To understand the impact, both positive and negative, that technology and the Internet has on the daily lives of people with disabilities, one must first have a general sense of how people with disabilities use and interact with such technologies. For individuals who are blind or visually impaired, the most commonly used means for connecting to the Internet and browsing the web are software applications that either magnify or enhance the text and images on the screen of the computer or hand-held device, read the text and images aloud through synthetic speech, or combine both of these approaches. To be effective, these applications need to operate in a predictable environment, meaning that the online destination to which a user goes must incorporate common design features with which these special applications can interact. When that environment is not so designed, the consequences can be devastating.

Take, for example, the case of Pam from Chicago who wrote to me in response to my invitation to share with this Subcommittee personal stories about the every-day online experiences of people with disabilities. As a mom who happens to be blind, Pam wants desperately to play as much of a role in the education of her son as would any loving parent. However, because the website used by her son's school system to allow parents the ability to track their children's progress, review teacher comments, and even peek at assignments that are in fact completed and grades received, does not incorporate basic web site accessibility design, Pam feels frustrated and ineffective as a parent. She of course is not an ineffective and uninvolved parent. She is, however, being shut out, through deliberate indifference by the school system that is aware of the website limitations, from her right as a parent to be fully involved with the education of her son. No half measures or alternative approaches that the school system might offer her can possibly afford Pam with the same degree of instant access, privacy, convenience and control over her ability to be a supportive and full partner in her son's education as is afforded parents who do not happen to have a disability. We can do better, and the promise of the ADA means that we must.

Try to imagine, if you can, how frustrating it is for people with vision loss to make the investment in frequently expensive specialized software and hardware for the express purpose of taking advantage of the world of possibilities open to anyone who can connect to the Internet only to find that much of what is available is just out of reach. Sophisticated software programs commonly used by people who are blind to read aloud the text on the computer screen can only work well when the websites visited allow them to do their job. My fellow panelists are certainly more well-versed than I about the technical requirements needed to ensure website accessibility, but I do know that the solutions to the most common website barriers are known and have been known for some time. The key is to incorporate accessible design at the earliest possible stage and not, as seems to be the case in Pam's situation, to leave accessibility as an afterthought.

Pat from California described her frustration with her bank which provides a website for customers to use to review statements and otherwise manage their accounts but which has failed to take accessibility into account. As she put it:

When I told my bank that I'm blind and can't use the website with my screen reader, they told me that they had heard that complaint before and that they knew it wasn't all that useful but that I could simply go over the information I was interested in by phone with them. I tried explaining to them that having them read through all the figures in my checking account over the phone would take forever and not let me see the information for myself, but they said that was the only option I had.

What Pat regularly experiences with her bank is an all-too-common problem. If Pat went into the bank and asked for help, and the bank refused outright to be of assistance to her, of course the ADA would give her a remedy. But in this instance, the bank is essentially saying that the first-class, up-to-date, information available to all customers will not be made available to Pat because they are providing inferior alternatives. That, of course, is the point. Increasingly, the web is providing more timely and accurate ways to manage our financial, health, and other data records—for all of us, that is, except too many people with disabilities. The ADA can, does, and must stand for the proposition that communication should be as effective for customers with disabilities as it is for those who do not have disabilities. In Pat's case, no alternative can afford the same degree of privacy, convenience, accuracy of information, and timeliness that the online statement and account management provides. Therefore, the promise of the ADA is only fulfilled when banks such as Pat's make their websites accessible.

John from Washington State emphasizes the online barriers to employment. He writes:

> An increasing number of individuals with disabilities seeking gainful employment into the nation's workforce continue to be significantly disadvantaged, and thereby left under or unemployed and reliant of the public safety net, because of the growing trend of online employment application processes, that are inaccessible to them. As an Employer Relations Manager ... in the State of Washington, it is brought to my attention constantly that employers have shifted their pre-employment process to the internet, that this shift has become very frustrating for job applicants with conditions such as blindness, deafness, reading disabilities, learning disabilities and many others. The lack of accessible application processes have an adverse impact on the desire of many qualified applicants to enter the labor force. We must do everything possible to increase the employment of people with disabilities, which includes removing the first barriers experienced in the hiring process.

John is right about a lot of things. He is right that making the Internet more accessible will have a direct impact on the ability of people with disabilities to obtain work and remain in the workforce. But he is also right in pointing out that web accessibility is not just a priority for people with vision loss. For example, people with motor difficulties or who may have cognitive disabilities frequently struggle to fill out online forms with built-in time-out features. Because the individual might not be able to complete the online form as quickly as might someone without those disabilities, the form "times out" and information entered is lost. Even many users without disabilities find this frustrating, but an accessibility solution that can be implemented allowing the user to opt out of the time-out function or to regularly save what information has been entered before the time runs out would be a tremendous help. The recognized web accessibility guidelines take such issues into account and, if implemented, would increase the usability of websites for many people with and without disabilities.

OPPORTUNITIES

In assessing trends in online shopping, comScore, Inc. (*www.comscore. com*) found that, in spite of a volatile economy, the 2009 November-December holiday season was a remarkable one for e-commerce with more than $29.1 billion in online retail spending reported. In fact, December 15, 2009, was an historic moment with the highest ever online spending in a single day, more than $913 million in sales. It is more than superfluous to say that e-commerce is booming and holds tremendous promise for business and customers alike. It is equally as clear that people with disabilities, either as employees, customers, or business owners can share in this potential but largely do not. As I have discussed and as my colleagues will further demonstrate, solutions currently exist that would, if more widely used, turn this unfortunate and unnecessary inequity around.

In fact, we know that this is already proving to be the case. Over the last few years, through measured advocacy, information sharing, and cooperative negotiation, several major companies, among them Marriott, CVS, RiteAid, and Radio Shack, have committed to making their websites much more accessible (See the impressive array of structured negotiation press releases at www.lflegal.com). What this important work shows is that companies committed to meeting the needs of all their customers can and do achieve what some nay-sayers allege cannot be done. Most recently, Major League Baseball has committed to making www.mlb.com fully accessible, making literally millions of fans of America's favorite pastime happy while demonstrating conclusively that significant progress toward an inclusive online world is within our reach.

More and more educational institutions are waking up to their responsibilities to ensure that students with and without disabilities can achieve academically by benefiting equally from the online learning tools and methods available. But even as we are pleased with the progress, we know there are many more opportunities to break down needless barriers to full participation by people with disabilities. As Claudia, a visually impaired veteran of the Persian Gulf War, explained it to me:

> I am currently enrolled in an online program with the University of Phoenix in the doctorate program for industrial and organizational psychology. I have noticed that the university goes through extensive efforts to make all forms of their online program accessible, however, this is not easily accomplished with copyrighted material for some scholarly articles provided through EBSCOHost, ProQuest, and Thomson Gayle databases. All of the databases are used by most libraries and provide extensive articles for research in any school projects. I have to spend numerous hours trying to get the articles to be accessible for me, therefore, I have to spend more hours and do lots of extra unnecessary steps to get the article. I think that companies make profits from universities, but never have any accountability for providing accessible documents to the university. ... I hope that your efforts are heard loudly and bring some accountability to those companies that use the internet to consider making the services accessible to all parties that could potentially use their services.

A STRATEGY FOR ENSURING DIGITAL INDEPENDENCE

What Claudia, John, Pat and Pam all know from their personal experiences and those of their family members, friends, coworkers, employees and clients, is that this question of the ADA's role in the digital age, as important as it is, cannot be considered in isolation. How do we, for example, ensure that a student who is blind can access her college's online portal from her mobile phone just like her classmates regularly do? How can we be sure, as online library websites are made accessible to more people with disabilities, that our copyright law rewards author and publisher creativity and investment while permitting all those with a right to read the materials to do so without artificial or unnecessary access barriers? How can we know for certain that a deaf couple will be able to rent and download movies from an online video store and have confidence that the captions provided with the original movie will be passed through to the couple's computer or Internet-equipped television? How we will ensure that people with vision loss have access to programs with description on televisions with controls they can independently use? And how will we know that the plentiful gadgets that hotels, universities, schools, conference centers, health facilities, and a host of other venues will increasingly offer, if not require us to use, will truly be usable by all of us?

The answer is that the DOJ's commitment to affirm and clarify the ADA's applicability to commercial websites is a critical component of a much larger policy agenda. The Congress can help to keep the ADA's promise of full inclusion by looking beyond the four corners of the ADA itself, beginning that commitment anew this year and promptly enacting H.R. 3101, the Twenty-first Century Communications and Video Accessibility Act. This landmark bipartisan legislation would ensure that mobile and other Internet-equipped devices and video technologies are accessible to and usable by people with disabilities. It makes no sense for us to praise ourselves for our commitment to the promise of the ADA if we fail to ensure that commonly available high tech tools are liberators and not liabilities for people with disabilities. There is no greater statement that the U.S. House could make this year to commemorate the twentieth anniversary of the ADA than the passage of H.R. 3101.

Additionally, the DOJ must take action to clarify that accessibility obligations under the ADA also extend to high-tech equipment. The DOJ must ensure that the pending refresh of the ADA regulations incorporates meaningful guidance to ADA covered entities with respect to their obligation to offer accessible equipment to patrons and customers. The proposed Title II and Title III regulations fail to address the need for accessibility to equipment provided by state and local government entities and public accommodations. Indeed, the regulations implementing the ADA have never adequately accounted for the need for access to equipment by people with disabilities, and the Department has acknowledged as much in the narrative accompanying the proposed regulations. For example, according to the Department,

> When the title III regulation was initially proposed in 1991, it contained a provision concerning accessible equipment, which required that newly purchased furniture or equipment that was made available for use at a place of public accommodation be accessible, unless complying with this requirement would fundamentally alter the goods, services, facilities, privileges, advantages, or accommodations offered, or would not be readily achievable. See 56 FR 7452, 7470-71 (Feb. 22, 1991). In the final title III regulation promulgated in 1991, the Department decided not to include this provision, explaining in the preamble to the regulation that 'its requirements are more properly addressed under other sections, and '... there are currently no appropriate accessibility standards addressing many types of furniture and equipment.' 56 FR 35544, 35572 (July 26, 1991). ' . . . The Department has

decided to continue with this approach, and not to add any specific regulatory guidance addressing equipment at this time.

Unfortunately, the other regulatory provisions that the Department says should address free standing equipment accessibility are at best vaguely applicable. They do not specifically mention equipment accessibility or provide examples of some of the most commonly used items.

As a result, ADA coverage for most of the equipment to which people with disabilities, such as people with vision loss, for example, need access is at best in doubt. There is no specific regulatory hook clearly requiring accessibility of, for example, exercise equipment using electronic interfaces, computers at Internet cafes or hotel business centers, reservations kiosks used by hotels in lieu of an in-person check in procedure, and devices provided by medical facilities with which a patient must interact reliably.

Sometimes making such equipment accessible can be as simple as labeling a few basic controls in braille or large print, and sometimes equipment accessibility demands the modification or purchase of additional software or hardware. The combined effect of miniaturization, reduced power consumption, increased memory and functional capacity, and ever-lowering costs, means that making electronic and information technology (E&IT) and other equipment utilizing visual displays accessible is significantly more accomplishable today than was the case when the original ADA regulations were published.

In spite of the fact that the Department is proposing not to address equipment accessibility, the Department is certainly aware of the issues. Remarkably, instead of spelling out additional regulatory requirements per se, the Department merely acknowledges in the narrative accompanying the proposed rules that,

> If a person with a disability does not have full and equal access to a covered entity's services because of the lack of accessible equipment, the entity must provide that equipment, unless doing so would be a fundamental alteration or would not be readily achievable.

We therefore urge the Department to specifically reference the accessibility of both fixed and free standing equipment in sections 36.302 and 36.304 entitled "Modifications in Policies, Practices, or Procedures" and "Removal of Barriers" respectively. The Department should reference specific examples of equipment (such as those outlined above) that best illustrate how such equipment's use is key to allowing people with disabilities to benefit from the goods and services offered by public accommodations such as private universities, hotels, medical facilities, gymnasia, business centers, retailers and others. Equipment accessibility is equally relevant in the context of Title II. Equipment such as automated teller machines, information kiosks and vending machines are frequently located in facilities operated by state and local government entities and hence, equipment accessibility should be addressed in the Title II regulations in a comparable manner to that which we propose for the Title III regulations.

CONCLUSION

In summary, we congratulate the DOJ for its leadership in ensuring the ADA's full relevance in the digital age. Hopefully the new rules will go a long way toward breaking down the often unseen but very real technology barriers that confront so many people with disabilities. We also know that much more needs to be done, and the American Foundation for the Blind is committed to working in partnership with you to expand possibilities for people with vision loss and all people with disabilities. Thank you.

In: Emerging Technology Issues for People...   ISBN: 978-1-61122-523-5
Editors: Daniel B. Bernardino   © 2011 Nova Science Publishers, Inc.

Chapter 5

STATEMENT OF JUDY BREWER, WEB ACCESSIBILITY INITIATIVE (WAI) AT THE WORLD WIDE WEB CONSORTIUM, BEFORE THE SUBCOMMITTEE ON THE CONSTITUTION, CIVIL RIGHTS, AND CIVIL LIBERTIES, HEARING ON "ACHIEVING THE PROMISE OF THE AMERICANS WITH DISABILITIES ACT IN THE DIGITAL AGE-CURRENT ISSUES, CHALLENGES AND OPPORTUNITIES"

Mr. Chairman, Members of the Committee, thank you for this opportunity to talk with you again regarding accessibility of the Web. My name is Judy Brewer, and I direct the Web Accessibility Initiative[i] (WAI) at the World Wide Web Consortium[ii] (W3C).

For the Web to work, computers need to be able to talk to each other across the Internet in the same computer languages – and W3C is where those languages are agreed upon. W3C is an international standards body with over 300 member organizations, primarily web industry leaders. We are based at the Massachusetts Institute of Technology, the European Research Consortium on Informatics and Mathematics in France, and Keio University in Japan. W3C is directed by Tim Berners-Lee, inventor of the Web, and a strong believer in the Web for All. W3C has developed over one hundred technical standards and guidelines, ranging from HTML and XML, to graphics, math, voice, rich media, mobile devices, web services, linked data, security, privacy, e-Government, internationalization, and more.

Among its other work, W3C hosts the Web Accessibility Initiative. WAI develops standards, guidelines and resources to make the Web accessible for people with disabilities; ensures accessibility of W3C technologies; and develops educational resources to support web accessibility. WAI is supported in part by the National Institute on Disability and Rehabilitation Research at the US Department of Education; the European Commission; WAI Sponsors; and W3C Member organizations. My comments do not necessarily represent those of WAI's funders.

Ten years ago this Subcommittee invited me to address early questions about web accessibility. A discussion that started with many myths and misperceptions concluded with a much clearer picture of the realities and promise of web accessibility.

In the intervening years:

- We've shown that businesses can flourish while producing accessible websites and services.
- We've shown that a multi-stakeholder process that includes industry, disability organizations, accessibility researchers and governments can develop consensus on web accessibility solutions.
- We've shown that accessibility solutions for people with different disabilities, including those with accessibility issues due to aging, are complementary, not conflicting, and are best achieved through a unified accessibility standard.
- We've developed guidelines and standards for web content, authoring tools, browsers, media players, and rich internet applications.
- In particular, we've shown that the Web Content Accessibility Guidelines (WCAG) 2.0:
  - are feasible for simple Mom & Pop websites, as well as for complex and dynamically-generated million-page websites;
  - are "technology neutral" – meaning that they can be applied to any web technology;
  - are more testable, yet support innovation;
  - have extensive, freely available technical support materials.

- Web developers from around the world have shown that accessible websites can be colorful, media-rich, dynamic, interactive, device independent, and international.

The Web has changed immensely in the past ten years. Many of our activities have moved to the Web – we get our education, jobs, health care, and tax forms online; buy music, clothes, and tickets; get our news, and not only buy but also read our books online. We use our mobile phones to do our banking, and our laptops to make phone calls. We do social networking with colleagues, family and friends. In contrast to ten years ago, many of these services exist only on the Web, through real-time transactions, yet are as vital to our social and economic life today as any bricks-and-mortar business of the past.

W3C's consensus-based standards development process, multi-stakeholder participation, broad public reviews, and implementation testing prior to finalization of standards have been an advantage to development of the Web as a whole, and equally to web accessibility. These processes have enabled the disability community to be present at the design table for web standards; to influence technologies that are newly moving onto the Web; and to influence accessibility of web-based interfaces as they move beyond the traditional Web into environments such as household devices and medical equipment. Development of accessibility solutions in a standards environment has ensured that web accessibility is consistent with and can evolve with the architecture of the Web. For technical communities outside of W3C and unused to the process of ensuring web accessibility in standards development, it has sometimes been a learning experience – yet this is also a reason why organizations seek out W3C as a standards development environment. W3C's accessibility guidelines respect the Web's capacity for innovation by providing a comprehensive and stable framework of principles, guidelines, and success criteria, with informative techniques to which developers can add and share innovations.

In 2008 this standards process produced the Web Content Accessibility Guidelines (WCAG) 2.0. The US Access Board has stated its intent to harmonize the web portions of its Section 508 regulations with WCAG 2. WCAG has been referenced in a Department of Justice ADA technical assistance manual, and in negotiated ADA settlements within the banking, retail and sports sectors. During the past year we've seen countries in Europe, as well Japan, Australia, New Zealand and many others move from other web accessibility standards to WCAG 2. This standards harmonization is immensely helpful because it creates a unified market and drives improvements in software, such as authoring tools, that can facilitate web accessibility.

Surveys of web accessibility progress continue to show barriers, the majority of which are due to failure to apply existing solutions – despite the good business case for web accessibility. Barriers include missing alternative text for images, missing captions for audio, forms that "time out" before you can submit them, images that flash and may cause seizures, text that moves or refreshes before you can interact with it, and websites that don't work with assistive technologies that many people with disabilities rely on. The impact on people with disabilities when there is a lack of accessibility ranges from exclusion from social networks, to missed school admissions, lost jobs, and inability to access life-saving health care information.

Opportunities to improve and accelerate web accessibility include:

- publishing existing data on the compliance of federal websites with Section 508 requirements, and conducting new studies that evaluate gaps in ADA compliance across Title II and Title III entities;
- communicating the applicability of the ADA to the Web more clearly, with updated guidance reflecting the benefits of standards harmonization at international, federal, and state levels;
- promoting development of improved authoring tools that facilitate the production of accessible web content, and that include accessible templates for website development;
- continuing research and development on accessibility techniques for new technologies, improved accessibility supports for cognitive disabilities, and more affordable assistive technologies.

The Web remains a springboard for innovation, exquisitely suited to support accessibility. Digital technology has already demonstrated how it can improve lives; let's make sure that people with disabilities are not excluded from its promise.

I would like to express my gratitude to the many hard-working participants and supporters around the world in the ongoing work on web accessibility; and my sincere thanks to the Subcommittee for your continued attention to accessibility of information technologies.

End Notes

[i] Web Accessibility Initiative http://www.w3.org/WAI/
[ii] World Wide Web Consortium http://www.w3.org/

In: Emerging Technology Issues for People...   ISBN: 978-1-61122-523-5
Editors: Daniel B. Bernardino   © 2011 Nova Science Publishers, Inc.

Chapter 6

STATEMENT OF STEVEN I. JACOBS, PRESIDENT, IDEAL GROUP, INC., BEFORE THE SUBCOMMITTEE ON THE CONSTITUTION, CIVIL RIGHTS AND CIVIL LIBERTIES, HEARING ON "ACHIEVING THE PROMISE OF THE AMERICANS WITH DISABILITIES ACT IN THE DIGITAL AGE-CURRENT ISSUES, CHALLENGES AND OPPORTUNITIES"

Mr. Chairman, Representative Nadler, and Representative Sensenbrenner, Ranking Member, and other Members of the Committee, thank you for this opportunity to present testimony on the current issues, challenges and opportunities in this digital age in regard to the Americans with Disabilities Act.

My name is Steve Jacobs. I have been in the computer industry for 35 years. As President of IDEAL Group[1], a 2002 spin-off from IDEAL at NCR Corporation[2] I have been intimately involved in the technological issues, challenges, and opportunities being discussed today.

As part of my testimony, I am going to show, by example, that there are alternatives to certain beliefs and concerns held by my industry colleagues at other IT companies.

Over the past 10 years our industry has experienced exponential growth which, on the surface, can appear to be exacerbating technology accessibility issues.

The number of internet users has risen from approximately 361 million[3] ten years ago to 1.8 billion[4] users at the end of 2009. This represents a 26.6% cumulative average growth rate. If this growth rate continues half the world's population will be using the internet by the end of 2012[5].

Web-based social networking communities are now frequented by over half-a-billion people every year[6].

4.1 billion SMS messages are being sent on a daily basis[7].

LinkedIn, an Internet-based business networking community has over 65 million members in 200 countries[8]. LinkedIn is accessible to a greater than lesser extent. Because of this, organizations of individuals with disabilities are able participate and interact with each other.

The number of organizations using web-delivered applications is increasing rapidly. There are 25 million users of Google applications[9].

There are 6,500 online college courses offered[10].

Shopping and making travel arrangements online is less expensive than brick-and-mortar alternatives. The trend in online learning is pointed upward.

Technology is woven into every aspect of life as we know it today. The ADA is about the civil rights of people with disabilities. When technology is inaccessible to people with disabilities seeking to access the same resources as their non-disabled counterparts... it violates their civil rights.

I manage four companies that market E&IT products and services. All of our products and services are accessible to people with disabilities. Designing accessible E&IT is easier, more technically possible, more economically feasible and more profitable to develop than ever before in history.

For example, up until recently, individuals who are blind had to pay $300-$400[11] extra for screenreading software in order to use a cell phone. Then along came Google Android[12] a free, open source, operating system for wireless smartphones. A smartphone is a mobile phone offering advanced capabilities, often with PC-like functionality. Thanks to innovative works of TV Raman and Charles Chen, two brilliant Google scientists and engineers, all Android smartphones come with a free screenreader and other accessibility applications. The iPhone[13] and iPad[14] also include free accessibility features. Google and Apple are not in business to lose money. They would not be integrating accessibility features into their smartphones for free if it were technically difficult, expensive or, if they lost money doing so.

Google provides the interfaces, development tools, platforms, marketing tools and distribution resources companies need to develop accessible applications[15]. Many accessibility applications have come on to the market[15a]. Our company formed Apps4Android[16], a Google smartphone application development company, in early 2009. In 14 short months our user base has grown to 600,000 users in 25 countries.

If our small company can be successful designing and selling accessible mainstream applications for this market, so can other companies. Wireless service providers, such as T-Mobile[17], have been open to learning more about potential opportunities in this space.

It used to be impractical to retrofit a web-based application to be accessible. That's no longer the case. Google AxsJAX[18] enables developers to create dynamically changing scripts that make their web applications more accessible. One of our subsidiary companies, IDEAL Conference[19], in partnership with Talking Communities has been provideding fully-accessible distance-learning, online conferencing and webinar services and accessibility training to hundreds of thousands of over the past eight years. Among those users are individuals with hearing impairments, people who are deaf, consumers with vision-loss, people with speech disabilities, persons with mobility disabilities and more.

It was reasonable, technically possible, economically feasible and profitable for us to do so. We are in business to make money. Just imagine the possibilities if large companies that currently market similar but inaccessible products and services would do the same.

Every minute, 20 hours of video are uploaded to YouTube. How can we expect every video owner to spend the time and effort necessary to add captions to their videos? Even with all of the captioning support already available a majority of user-generated video content online is still inaccessible to people who are deaf.

Ken Harrenstien a Google Software Engineer recently combined Google's automatic speech recognition (ASR) technology with the YouTube caption system to offer automatic captions, or auto-caps for short.

Auto-caps use the same voice recognition algorithms in *Google* to automatically generate captions for video. While the captions may not always be perfect they can still be incredibly helpful, and the technology will continue to improve with time. If implementing these technologies were not technically possible, economically feasible and profitable, Google would not be evolving them.

Partners for the initial launch of auto-caps are UC Berkeley, MIT, Yale, UCLA, Duke, UCTV, Columbia, PBS, National Geographic, Demand Media, UNSW, and most Google and YouTube channels[20].

In addition to automatic captions Google is also launching automatic caption timing, or auto-timing, to make it significantly easier to create captions manually. With auto-timing, you no longer need to have special expertise to create your own captions for YouTube videos. All you'll need to do is create a simple text file with all the words in the video and use Google's ASR technology to figure out when the words are spoken and create captions for your video. This should significantly lower the barriers for video owners who want to add captions, but who don't have the time or resources to create professional caption tracks[20]. Talk about technically possible and economically feasible!

Our National Broadband Plan[21] is shaping the future of issues that matter to all of us. Broadband networks and applications are critical to the competitive advantage and future success of our country. Broadband will serve as the platform to stimulate the creation of innovative business, education, government, entertainment and social online products and services. Health-focused broadband applications will transform health care. All patients will want to exercise their legal and civil rights to obtain personal health records, interact with physician offices, obtain lab results, schedule appointments... and much more... all online.

We've known it for a long time: the web is big. The first Google index in 1998 already had 26 million pages, and by 2000 the Google index reached the one billion mark. Google has now indexed far in excess of one trillion unique URLs[22]. Internet users conduct over two billion Google searches every day[23].

Georgia Tech's sonification lab[24] is using free, open source, software developed by NASA Learning Technologies[25] to create fully-accessible, free, web-based resources designed to enable the participation and enhance the performance of America's students with print disabilities in science, technology, engineering, and mathematics (STEM)[26]. This include efforts not only from the Federal Government but also from leading companies, foundations, non-profits, and science and engineering societies. These organizations would not be making the commitments of technology and resources if achieving these technology objectives were technically impossible, economically unfeasible or would cost a lot of money... especially in today's economy.

Thanks to Dr. Margo Izzo a researcher at The Nisonger Center at The Ohio State University[27] and talented software developers from around the world, students with disabilities are now being provided with free, portable, high-quality, assistive technology software smartdrives to benefit students with disabilities in the following ways:

- Enables students attending any school/university to use their AT software on practically any PC they desire/need to use;
- Significantly reduces the cost of providing AT software to students who desire/need to use it;
- Reduces incompatibility/interoperability issues with applications currently installed on the PC being used;
- Eliminates vandalism and innocent corruptions of PC-based AT software since portable AT applications are not installed on the PC being used. Students simply carry their AT software, personal files, and configuration files with them;
- Eliminates licensing limitations that preclude students from using AT software on any PC they desire/need to use;
- Eliminates the problem of too few AT software-equipped computers in schools, colleges, libraries, community centers, places of employment etc.;
- Improves transition outcomes for AT software users from school to school, high school to college, high school to employment and in adult life in general;
- Eliminates financial losses due to AT software abandonment;
- Eliminates acquisition time and red tape;
- Eliminates installation problems; and,
- Eliminates the stigma of having to use "special" PCs.

IDEAL Group is looking forward to exploring the possibilities of distributing our assistive technology software smartdrives though State Assistive Technology Act (ATAP) Programs, funded under the AT Act of 1998, as amended.

In closing, I encourage all of you not to permit the sometimes exaggerated perceptions of technology accessibility issues and challenges cloud the fact that there are now more opportunities than ever before in history to design accessible and profitable E&IT products and services.

All of you on this subcommittee are in the enviable position to help every person, regardless of ability, be able to exercise their civil rights by having equal access to E&IT.

There is additional information in PowerPoint format, as part of this testimony, at the end of this written statement.

Thank you!

About IDEAL Group, Inc.
Steve Jacobs, President
IDEAL Group, Inc.
2809 Bohlen Drive
Hilliard, Ohio 43026
Phone: (614) 777-0660
TTY/TDD: (800) 750-0750
steve.jacobs@ideal

IDEAL Group, Inc. is a 2002 spin-off from IDEAL at NCR Corporation (NYSE: NCR). IDEAL Group has four subsidiary companies:

1. Online Conferencing Systems Group, *Inc.*
    http://onlineconferencingsystems.com
    Online Conferencing Systems Group provides fully accessible, 508 compliant, online conferencing, distance learning and Webinar services. OCSG has served hundreds-of-thousands of users worldwide over the past eight years.
2. InftyReader Group, Inc.
    http://www.inftyreader.org
    InftyReader Group provides applications that recognize and translates science, technology, engineering, and math (STEM) documents into accessible formats for individuals with print disabilities. See our Accessible math resource: http://www.accessiblemath.org/ See our Speech Recognition-Based Math Accessibility Project: http://inftyreader.org/speech
3. Apps4Android, Inc.
    http://apps4android.org
    Apps4Android is a Google Android smartphone assistive technology software development company. Apps4Android is dedicated to developing free/low-cost, high-quality, mobile applications that enhance the quality-of-life, independence and employability of

individuals with disabilities. After only 14 months in business, Apps4Android applications are being used by more than 600,000 users in 25+ countries. See our Android Accessibility Project: http://accessibility.

4. EasyCC, Inc.
http://easycc.org/
EasyCC is the newest IDEAL Group subsidiary company. EasyCC provides real-time captioning services to organizations wishing to accommodate the access needs of individuals who are deaf.

REFERENCES

[1] History of IDEAL Group: http://www.ideal
[2] NCR Corporation website: http://www.ncr.com/
[3] 361 million: http://www.internetworldstats.com/stats.htm
[4] 1.8 billion: http://www.internetworldstats.com/stats.htm
[5] 1.8B x 126.6 x 126.6 x 126.6 = 3.65B
[6] Social networking statistics:
Facebook: http://tinyurl.com/356y6s
Twitter: http://tinyurl.com/y9dm7sh
MySpace: http://tinyurl.com/y4fk6rm
[7] 4.1 billion: http://tinyurl.com/y4n86vm
[8] LinkedIn: http://press.linkedin.com/about
[9] Google apps: http://tinyurl.com/yyqd3pq
[10] Online courses: http://www.elearners.com/courses/
[11] Nuance TALKS: http://tinyurl.com/y74zh97Mobile Speak: *http://tinyurl.com/y5979gg*
[12] Google Android: http://www.android.com/
[13] iPhone accessibility: http://tinyurl.com/6optfu
[14] iPad Accessibility: http://tinyurl.com/yfw54rv
[15] Android Market: http://www.android.com/market/15a. *http://www.accessibility-android.info/stats.htm*
[16] Apps4Android: http://apps4android.org
[17] T-Mobile: http://tinyurl.com/yybvqh8
[18] Google AxsJAX: http://tinyurl.com/yysav2m
[19] IDEAL Conference: http://onlineconferencingsystems.com
[20] Google Captions: http://tinyurl.com/ykzj44a

[21]   National Broadband Plan: http://www.broadband.gov/
[22]   Google indexed websites: http://tinyurl.com/5blvgm
[23]   Google Searches: http://tinyurl.com/9oo4te
[24]   Georgia Tech's Sonification Lab: http://sonify.psych.gatech.edu/
[25]   NASA Learning Technologies: http://tinyurl.com/y37l22r
[26]   Educate to Innovate: http://tinyurl.com/yb3sjr3
[27]   Nisonger Center: http://nisonger.osu.edu/
[28]   ATAP: http://www.ataporg.org/atap/index.php

In: Emerging Technology Issues for People...   ISBN: 978-1-61122-523-5
Editors: Daniel B. Bernardino   © 2011 Nova Science Publishers, Inc.

Chapter 7

STATEMENT OF DANIEL F. GOLDSTEIN, ESQ., PARTNER, BROWN, GOLDSTEIN & LEVY, LLP, BEFORE THE SUBCOMMITTEE ON THE CONSTITUTION, CIVIL RIGHTS AND CIVIL LIBERTIES, HEARING ON "ACHIEVING THE PROMISE OF THE AMERICANS WITH DISABILITIES ACT IN THE DIGITAL AGE-CURRENT ISSUES, CHALLENGES AND OPPORTUNITIES"

Mr. Chairman, members of the Committee, thank you for inviting me here today. As a partner in the Baltimore, Maryland law firm of Brown, Goldstein & Levy, LLP, I have been engaged in disability rights law, principally on behalf of the National Federation of the Blind ("NFB"), since 1986. In 1999, the NFB asked me to assist it in devising a strategy to promote the accessibility of digital information through education, negotiation and litigation. I have devoted much of the last 11 years to that effort.

The ADA has played a valuable role in that undertaking, as we have worked to make websites, workplace software applications, ATMs, voting machines, cell phones and e-book reading devices accessible to people with vision and print disabilities.

The challenge is immense. Digital information is everywhere, from consumer electronics and home appliances to the internet, computer screens and mobile devices to ticket kiosks and ATMs. It is difficult to identify an activity in modern American life in which digital information does not play a role.

Because digital information is composed of zeros and ones, it is not inherently visual, aural or tactile but can be presented in any one or all of those modes with equivalent facility. Thus, the ubiquitous use of digital information should be great news for those who cannot access print because of a disability – whether it's a vision disability, a learning disability, an intellectual disability, or a manual impairment or spinal cord injury. Similarly, digital information that was traditionally presented as speech can now produce mainstream accessibility for those with hearing impairments.

Sadly, however, the potential for the disability community to have mainstream and therefore equal access has not been realized. So much electronic information is presented so that it is accessible only to one sense, resulting in persons with disabilities having unequal access and therefore being denied the opportunity for equal participation in all spheres of life. Thus, to give you a homely example, something as simple as setting the thermostat in one's house, which a blind person could formerly do by adding tactile markings to the dial that controlled the thermostat, is now an inaccessible activity. Even though digital temperature controls could communicate both visually and audibly, most provide only visual information, leaving blind people worse off than before.

A. THE ADA AND PUBLIC ACCOMMODATION WEBSITES

The ADA is key to unlocking these doors. Title III of the ADA applies to public accommodations, defined as 12 categories of commercial entities that interact with the public. We believe both the intent and the language of the ADA cover websites and other digital information and services provided by those covered entities, regardless of whether those entities also operate brick-and-mortar locations.

In 1999, on behalf of the NFB, I filed suit in federal court in Massachusetts against America Online for violating Title III of the ADA by failing to make its service accessible to the blind. The First Circuit had held in the context of insurance services that a public accommodation may be covered under Title III of the ADA without the activity being linked to a physical place of public accommodation. We were anxious to follow that case law to its logical conclusion that websites that offer the services of a public accommodation, as delineated in Title III, are likewise covered by the ADA. However, AOL quickly decided to make its website fully accessible, so the matter was settled without creating any judicial precedent.

In 2006, we filed suit against the Target Corporation over the inaccessibility of its website. After the federal court in San Francisco ruled that the portions of the website that had a nexus to the physical stores were covered by the ADA,[1] Target settled and has since made its website fully accessible.[2]

Opponents of the application of Title III to commercial and educational websites might argue that some federal case law supports the proposition that e-commerce is outside the scope of the ADA. There is a line of reasoning adopted in some circuits that a place of public accommodation, within the meaning of Title III, must be an "actual, physical" place.[3] These courts have held that to state a claim under Title III, the plaintiff must allege either that there has been discrimination in a physical place, or that there is a "nexus" between the challenged act of discrimination and a physical place of public accommodation. This approach stands in stark contrast to the more commonsense view adopted by several other circuits that the phrase "public accommodation" encompasses more than just physical structures.[4]

Most cases addressing the "place" argument have been in the context of insurance, considering whether the ADA's non-discrimination requirements govern the substance of insurance policies. None of the circuit courts adopting the "physical place" line of reasoning have addressed the precise question of whether public accommodations that operate through the internet or its websites are places of public accommodation under Title III. So we do not currently know what conclusion these circuits would reach on that issue.

In today's increasingly online society, limiting the ADA (or any civil rights law) to only those businesses that operate in physical facilities would undermine the fundamental goals of civil rights. Given that one of the essential purposes of Title III is to eliminate discrimination against people with disabilities in the basic, day-to-day activities that are a fundamental part of living and functioning in a community, it is hard to imagine that coverage would depend on whether a covered entity offers its services and goods in a physical location, door-to-door, by phone, or online. In an age where hundreds of millions of Americans are increasingly using the internet every day to shop for groceries, plan their travel, conduct business, do their banking, attend college classes, and socialize with friends and family, it is undeniable that these websites are an indispensable part of basic, day-to-day life in the community.

Despite this obvious reality of life in the internet era, one district court, in *Access Now v. Southwest Airlines Co.* has erroneously extended the "physical place" line of reasoning to conclude that it would not apply Title III to prohibit discriminatory access to Southwest's website where the plaintiff had failed to allege a "nexus" between the site and a physical, brick-and-mortar place.[5] I have no doubt that the district court's interpretation of Title III in the *Southwest* case was incorrect, and that a federal Court of Appeals squarely presented with the issue should reach the conclusion that Title III applies to goods and services provided over the internet. But the fact that the district court strayed so far from Title III's fundamental purpose was troubling, and is one of the reasons that I applaud the Committee's decision to hold this hearing.

In light of Assistant Attorney General Perez's affirmation last week that the Department of Justice continues to believe that public accommodations are covered by Title III even when they reach the public only via websites, it seems to me that the time has come to test this proposition in the courts as well as through the development of regulations by the Department of Justice.

Court cases aside, in the years since the internet has become a mainstay of American life, some advocates and covered entities have reached agreements about accessibility of internet sites. Among the websites that have reached such agreements, variously, with the NFB, the American Council of the Blind and the New York and Massachusetts Offices of Attorney General are: Amazon.com, Apple's iTunes, Major League Baseball, CVS, Radio Shack, Rite Aid, Staples, Ramada Hotels, and Priceline.com. Other companies with commercial websites have reached out proactively to secure certification from the NFB that their websites are accessible, including both large companies like G.E. and NewEgg and small businesses like my law firm.

These agreements and the *Target* case have had a positive impact in increasing website accessibility across the commercial industry. A study of the top thirty-two online retailers' websites that analyzed the websites' accessibility one year before the *Target* decision and one year following the decision found a significant improvement in overall accessibility.[6]

Using the standards and tools provided by the ADA, we are seeing voice-guided ATMs and Accessible Point-of-Sale Machines. In the case of the former, with the recent announcement by Bank of America that all of its ATMs now have voice-guidance and my settlement with the largest nonbank deployer of ATMs, Cardtronics, inaccessible ATMs are becoming the exception rather than the rule.

ATMs, however, provide an important lesson. The technology to make ATMs accessible is older than the technology to make ATMs and the additional cost of accessibility in manufacturing and deploying ATMs is marginal. However, delay by banks and other deployers of ATMs to comply with the ADA until the national fleet of ATMs was mature led to a tremendous and unnecessary increase in costs in retrofitting or replacing functioning inaccessible ATMs. It also needlessly delayed the blind from having this convenience that so many rely on.

When new technologies find acceptance in the marketplace, their adoption and improvement often occurs with dizzying speed. When accessibility is not built in from the outset, however, the disability community suffers significant competitive disadvantages whose later correction may come only as that technology is being replaced by something newer or better. When a Microsoft offers first Windows Vista and then Windows 7 that were accessible from the day each went on the market, or Apple develops, as it has, a technology that allows the controls of its iPad to be accessible to the blind, this is cause for celebration.

The list of other technologies that have been accessible from their entry into the market, however, remains far too short. Gratuitous barriers to accessibility are still the rule, not the exception. Improved clarity about the application of the ADA to public accommodations operating over the internet will help. As is demonstrated by the experience of educational institutions, once the purchasers of technology understand their obligations and insist on accessibility by their suppliers, accessibility becomes mainstreamed.

B. INACCESSIBLE DIGITAL INFORMATION IN EDUCATION

Nowhere is the impact of digital information felt more than in the field of education. The impact is pronounced here, perhaps more than in any other sphere because digital information and electronic technology have the potential to change the game for students with print disabilities. However, educational institutions are not meeting that potential. For example, a 2008 study that examined the accessibility of postsecondary education web pages found that 97% of the institutions in its sample contained significant accessibility barriers.[7] The study examined only top or home pages of university websites, suggesting that the significant barriers are even more deeply entrenched than indicated by the study.

That the vast majority of educational institutions fail to recognize their obligations under the ADA to make their website information accessible is only the tip of the iceberg. Reliance on online education is steeply increasing, with online enrollments growing substantially faster than overall higher education enrollments in the past six years.[8] Meanwhile, digital books, course management systems, and other educational technologies have become an integral part of post-secondary education. Many of these technologies are completely – and gratuitously – inaccessible to students and others with print disabilities.

While universities and institutions have often failed to appreciate their obligations under the ADA and their commercial power as consumers of educational technology, some positive examples of success demonstrate the kind of impact institutions can have if their obligations under the ADA are made clear and enforceable.

i. Universities and Amazon's Kindle DX

In February 2009, the Kindle 2 was introduced with a read-out-loud feature, but with on-screen navigation that was not voiced and was therefore inaccessible to the blind. The Association of American Publishers and the Authors Guild sought to have Amazon terminate this feature. In response, the Reading Rights Coalition was formed, thirty-two nonprofits representing the print-disability community—including, among others, the blind, people with dyslexia and other learning disabilities, those with cerebral palsy, and those with upper spinal cord injuries. The Coalition worked on one hand to protect the inclusion of Text-to-Speech while fighting to have Amazon allow its menus to talk and thus make the device accessible.

In May 2009, Amazon announced the launch of its Kindle DX e-book reader, which it had designed for educational use. Because Amazon failed to include accessible navigational controls, the device was inaccessible to the blind. Six colleges and universities simultaneously announced they would be deploying the Kindle DX during the 2009 – 2010 academic year. The National Federation of the Blind and the American Council of the Blind filed a complaint in federal court against Arizona State University and filed complaints with the Department of Justice and Department of Education against the remaining schools (Pace University, Case Western Reserve

University, Reed College, Princeton University, and the University of Virginia's Darden School of Business). These complaints alleged that by deploying the inaccessible Kindle, the colleges and universities violated their obligations under Titles II and III of the ADA to provide equal access to their services. While sighted students would benefit from the instant access, notetaking, and other services of the Kindle, blind students would be left behind, forced to rely on separate methods of access that are significantly inferior to even the print textbook experience. The complaint against the University of Virginia is still pending with the Department of Education, but the NFB, the ACB and the Department of Justice secured settlements with the other five schools under which those schools agreed, after the end of this semester, not to deploy inaccessible e-book readers.

While those complaints were pending, other universities stepped forward to publicly pledge they would not adopt e-book technologies on their campus – including the Kindle – unless and until they were accessible. Those universities included Syracuse University, the University of Wisconsin and the University of Illinois. In response to this pressure, Amazon announced that it would release a fully accessible Kindle in the summer of 2010. And on March 9, 2010, the Reading Rights Coalition, the Association of American Publishers and the Authors Guild issued a joint statement, released on the White House blog, supporting mainstream accessibility when books are issued in formats other than print, such as e-books and audio books.[9]

ii. Libraries and Adobe Digital Editions

Adobe Digital Editions is the leading commercial e-book format used by libraries and also the format that can be read on the inaccessible Sony e-book reader. Until March 2009, Adobe e-books had been accessible to those who require speech to access text and who downloaded those books to a PC. In March 2009, however, Adobe stopped support of that accessible system and switched to a new, inaccessible e-book platform, called Adobe Digital Editions. As a result, numerous public library patrons with disabilities could no longer access their libraries' digital collections.

Advocacy from the Burton Blatt Institute and the Reading Rights Coalition prompted the American Library Association to adopt a resolution strongly recommending that libraries ensure that all electronic resources they procure are accessible to people with disabilities.[10] Shortly thereafter, the Los Angeles Public Library, responding to a letter from the Reading Rights

Coalition, agreed to suspend future procurement of Adobe Digital Editions books until they are fully accessible.[11] In response, Adobe announced that it would release an accessible Adobe Digital Editions in 2010.[12] Thus, when institutional customers of technology, like libraries, act on their obligations under the ADA, the developers of those technologies find strong economic motivation to remove the barriers to accessibility.

iii. California State University and BlackBoard

California State University succeeded in moving one of the leading course-management software systems, BlackBoard Learn, toward accessibility. In the late-1990's, the Department of Education's Office of Civil Rights launched an investigation into California State University campuses' compliance with, among other statutes, Title II of the ADA. In response, the Cal State system revamped its approach to providing access to students with disabilities and has become a leader and model for educational institutions to follow. Specifically, rather than delegating accessibility obligations to an isolated Disability Student Services office, as most universities do, Cal State established a system-wide, coordinated approach to accessibility. Under this approach, accessibility experts work closely with the University's information officers to ensure that the technology the university employs is accessible.

Through this arrangement, Cal State requires that new technologies it procures be accessible to its students. When Cal State put out a request for proposals for new course management software, it turned down BlackBoard – the leading purveyor of course management software – because it did not meet Cal State's accessibility requirements. Since that time, BlackBoard has issued two new releases of its software that greatly enhance its accessibility.[13]

C. THE NEXT STEPS TO ACCESS TO TECHNOLOGY

We are not even halfway there on making the internet accessible and in making accessible the technologies used in the workplace and offered through public accommodations, like educational institutions. And, of course, new technologies continue to develop and flourish with astonishing speed. The barriers to accessibility, however, are not the result, for the most part, of intractable technological issues and need not (and as a practical matter, would not) slow down innovation. The biggest contributor to the growing accessibility gap continues to be a lack of commitment to making technology accessible.

The ADA was a tremendous normative statement of the importance we attach as a nation to equal opportunity without regard to disability. But while the disability community has the responsibility to use the ADA and the other tools offered by federal and state laws, government must continue to make clear its commitment to that promise as well. The National Broadband Plan, for example, states as one of its goals that "every American should have affordable access to robust broadband service, and the means and skills to subscribe if they so choose."[14] It envisions, among other things "improvements in public education through e-learning and online content" and improvements in health care through the expansion of "e-care."[15] Without concrete steps to build in accessibility at every stage and level, this promise to "every American" will not be realized. Recognizing this, the National Broadband Plan specifically states that "hardware, software, services and digital content must be accessible and assistive technologies must be affordable."[16] The Plan calls on the federal government to be a model of accessibility, to specifically support innovation in accessibility, and to clarify and modernize its accessibility laws, enforcement efforts, and subsidy programs. In that respect, the federal government has a long way to go, as it has failed to monitor and enforce the provisions of Section 508 of the Rehabilitation Act.

The National Education Technology Plan, currently in draft form, addresses to some degree the need for Education Technology to be designed for mainstream accessibility for those with disabilities and we hope the final draft will be more robust. However, recent draft rules regarding Health Information Technology fail to wholeheartedly incorporate accessibility. Again, the federal government must make sure that the execution follows the good intentions.

Our milestones under the ADA thus far have been significant, but we remain far behind where we ought to be in an era that relies so intrinsically upon digital information. The near future will only expedite the transition to digital information in critical sectors – including education, employment, health care, commerce and social life. If we do not ensure that people with disabilities have equal access to digital information, they face exclusion from participation in our society.

The commitment we have already seen from the Department of Justice will take us nearer that goal. The Department of Education, Department of Health and Human Services, General Services Administration, Federal

Communications Commission, and others have important opportunities to advance accessible technology as well. There are good reasons to believe that the disability community, acting for itself and with the support of governmental entities, can make great strides toward the day that it no longer must settle for separate and unequal access to technology, but will have, instead, the same access to mainstream technology and thus an equal opportunity to participate in the educational, economic and social life of this country.

Thank you

End Notes

[1] *Nat'l Fed'n of the Blind v. Target Corp.*, 452 F.Supp.2d 946 (N.D. Cal 2006).

[2] *Nat'l Fed'n of the Blind, v. Target Corp.*, No. 3:06-cv-01802-MHP Doc. 210 (N.D. Cal. Mar. 9, 2008) (final judgment and order approving settlement and dismissing claims).

[3] *See Weyer v. Twentieth Century Fox Film Corp.*, 198 F.3d 1104, 1114 (9th Cir. 2000) (concluding that places of public accommodation are "actual, physical places."); *see also Ford v. Schering-Plough Corp.*, 145 F.3d 601, 612–13 (3d Cir. 1998) (holding that plaintiff failed to allege a nexus between the place of public accommodation and the insurance benefits offered by the employer); *Stoutenborough v. National Football League*, 59 F.3d 580, 583–84 (6th Cir. 1995) (affirming the dismissal of a claim under Title III because the challenged service, the live telecast of a football game, was not offered by a place of public accommodation, the stadium).

[4] *See Carparts Distribution Ctr., Inc. v. Automotive Wholesalers Assoc. of New England, Inc.*, 37 F.3d 12, 19–20 (1st Cir. 1994) (holding that "public accommodations" encompasses more than actual physical structures and includes the defendant insurance company); *Doe v. Mutual of Omaha Ins. Co.*, 179 F.3d 557, 559 (7th Cir. 1999) (noting that a "place of public accommodation" encompasses facilities open to the public in both physical and electronic space, including websites).

[5] *Access Now, Inc. v. Southwest Airlines Co.*, 227 F.Supp.2d 1312 (2002). On appeal, the 11th Circuit dismissed the appeal without reaching the merits of the case, so the 11th Circuit has not yet addressed the issue. *See Access Now, Inc. v. Southwest Airlines Co.*, 385 F. 3d 1324 (11th Cir. 2004).

[6] Jonathan Frank, "Web Accessibility for the Blind: Corporate Social Responsibility? or Litigation Avoidance?," pp.284, Proceedings of the 41st Annual Hawaii International Conference on System Sciences (HICSS 2008), 2008.

[7] Project GOALS Evaluates 100 Pages in Higher Education for Accessibility Against Section 508 Standard, NCDAE Newsletter, April 2008. Retrieved: http://ncdae.org/community/newsletter/april2008/

[8] I. Elaine Allen and Jeff Seaman, Learning on Demand: Online Education in the United States, 2009, Babson Survey Research Group, January 2010. Retrieved at: http://www.sloan-c.org/publications/survey

[9] http://www.whitehouse.gov/blog/2010/03/09/one-step-closer-full-access

[10] Purchasing of Accessible Electronic Resources Resolution, American Library Association, July 15, 2009. Retrieved at: *http://bbi.syr.edu/events/ 2009/docs/ Purchasing_Accessible_ Electronic_Resources_Resolution_revised_52.doc.*

[11] Letter to Eve Hill from Martin Gomez, August 31, 2009. http://www.readingrights.org/477

[12] Bill McCoy, Adobe eBooks - Update on Accessibility Support, October 8, 2009. http://blogs

[13] National Federation of the Blind and Blackboard to Demonstrate New Accessibility Features at CSUN, March 25, 2010. http://www.nfb.org/nfb/NewsBot.asp?MODE=VIEW&ID=566

[14] http://www.broadband.gov/plan/executive-summary/ ("National Broadband Plan").

[15] *Id.*

[16] National Broadband Plan at 181 ("Addressing Issues of Accessibility for Broadband Adoption and Utilization").

In: Emerging Technology Issues for People...   ISBN: 978-1-61122-523-5
Editors: Daniel B. Bernardino   © 2011 Nova Science Publishers, Inc.

Chapter 8

OVER THE HORIZON: POTENTIAL IMPACT OF EMERGING TRENDS IN INFORMATION AND COMMUNICATION TECHNOLOGY ON DISABILITY POLICY AND PRACTICE

National Council on Disability

EXECUTIVE SUMMARY

The technologies used in information and communication products are advancing at an ever increasing rate. Devices are getting smaller, lighter, cheaper, and more capable. Electronics are being incorporated into practically everything, making a wide variety of products programmable, and thus more flexible. Computing power is increasing exponentially. What requires a supercomputer one year can be done on a child's game player 15 years later.

There are many emerging technology trends that affect technologies used by people with disabilities. Four that will have particular impact on information and communication technologies (ICT) are:

- Increasing computational power, combined with decreasing size and costs;

- New interface research in areas such as virtual projected interfaces, speech input and output, direct brain interfaces, multi modal interfaces, and artificial intelligent agents that can act as mediators;
- Ubiquitous connectivity and network services, including the ability to be in constant connection with people or services that can provide assistance or augment a person's abilities – all with technologies that soon will be wearable or incorporated directly into clothing; and
- Creation of virtual places, service providers, and products that can enable a person to shop, explore, learn, travel, socialize, and work in "cyber space."

New Opportunities

These technical advances will provide a number of opportunities for improvement in the daily lives of individuals with disabilities, including work, education, travel, entertainment, healthcare, and independent living.

It is becoming much easier to make mainstream products more accessible. The increasing flexibility and adaptability that technology advances bring to mainstream products will make it more practical and cost effective to build accessibility directly into these products, often in ways that increase their mass market appeal. Although products have been getting progressively more complex for some time now, advances in key technologies will soon make it possible to reverse that trend and make products simpler. Improvements in connectivity and interoperability will enable individuals with severe or multiple disabilities, who could not operate the standard interface on universally designed products, to use products via a personal interface device that matches their abilities.

Less costly and more effective assistive technologies (AT) will also be possible as technology advances. More importantly, however, emerging technologies will enable the development of new types of AT, including technologies that can better address the needs of individuals with language, learning, and some types of cognitive disabilities. A potential for new "intelligent AT" is emerging that was previously not possible. Translating and transforming technologies will be able to take information that is not perceivable or understandable to many with sensory or cognitive impairments, and render it into a form that they can use. Human augmentation technologies will enhance some individuals' basic abilities, enabling them to better deal with the world as they encounter it. Advances in technology will also reduce the size and cost of products, making them easier to carry, wear, and, in some instances, replace. Assistive devices will be made available to and usable by those who would not have used them in the past out of a concern that they might lose them.

Barriers, Concerns, and Issues

Many of the same technological advances that show great promise of improved accessibility, however, also have the potential to create new barriers for people with disabilities. The following are some emerging technology trends that are causing accessibility problems.

- Devices will continue to get more complex to operate before they get simpler. This is already a problem for mainstream users, but even more of a problem for individuals with cognitive disabilities and people who have cognitive decline due to aging.
- Increased use of digital controls (e.g., push buttons used in combination with displays, touch screens, etc.) is creating problems for individuals with blindness, cognitive and other disabilities.
- The shrinking size of products is creating problems for people with physical and visual disabilities.
- The trend toward closed systems, for digital rights management or security reasons, is preventing individuals from adapting devices to make them accessible, or from attaching assistive technology so they can access the devices.
- Increasing use of automated self-service devices, especially in unattended locations, is posing problems for some, and absolute barriers for others.
- The decrease of face-to-face interaction, and increase in e-business, e-government, e-learning, e-shopping, etc., is resulting in a growing portion of our everyday world and services becoming inaccessible to those who are unable to access these Internet-based places and services.

In addition, the incorporation of new technologies into products is causing products to advance beyond current accessibility techniques and strategies. The rapid churn of mainstream technologies, that is, the rapid replacement of one product by another, is so fast that assistive technology developers cannot keep pace. Even versions of mainstream technologies that happen to be accessible to a particular group can quickly churn back out of the marketplace. To complicate the situation further, the convergence of functions is accompanied by a divergence of implementation. That is, products increasingly perform multiple functions that were previously performed by separate devices, but these "converged" products are using different (and often incompatible) standards or methods to perform the functions. This can have a negative effect on interoperability between AT and mainstream technology where standards and requirements are often weak or nonexistent. Thus, without action, the gap between the mainstream technology products being introduced and the assistive technologies necessary to make them accessible will increase, as will the numbers of technologies for which no accessibility adaptations are available.

Another concern is that technology advances are causing functions and product types to develop beyond the scope of existing policy. For example, when telephony moved from the public switched telephone network (PSTN) to the Internet, the accessibility regulations did not keep pace. The FCC determined that the Internet was information technology, and that the access regulations apply only to telecommunications, even though people were using the same phones and the same household wiring to make phone calls to the same people, many of whom were on the PSTN. Although the FCC has recently applied some telecommunications policies – namely those requiring E-9-1-1 call handling, electronic surveillance, and contributions to the Universal Service Fund – to some IP services, most of the remaining telecommunications regulations, including those requiring accessibility, have not been applied to these new technologies. Internet Protocol Television (IPTV) manufacturers are now talking about including conversation capabilities in their base technologies, again raising the question as to whether telecommunication accessibility will apply to these "phone calls." When accessibility is tied to technologies that become obsolete, often to be replaced by multiple new technologies, the accessibility requirements are often late or deemed not applicable. The shift of education, retail sales, etc. to the Internet after the ADA was drafted resulted in the Internet versions of these activities not being specifically mentioned in the law. This is another example of policy not keeping pace with technology. The evolving technology(s) involving copyright and digital rights management is another example.

The issue of policy not keeping pace with technology and product advances, however, goes beyond accessibility regulations. It can also apply to funding and eligibility issues. Often, the result is that people with disabilities become trapped, using old technologies that no longer work in their environment and activities.

Finally, there should be a broader recognition of the importance of having a "business case" for accessibility. This report focuses on new technologies and how they can benefit people with disabilities. None of these technologies will benefit people with disabilities unless they are built into products, made available, and supported. And none of that will occur in any reliable and sustainable fashion unless individuals within companies can make a business case for each new feature. Net profit is the primary reason products make it to the marketplace and remain there, and the primary reason ideas carry forward from one version of a product to other products. This is not specific to disability issues. It applies to all products. If a goal of our society is to have products that are accessible to and usable by people with disabilities, then mechanisms are needed to make accessible products generate significantly more net revenue for a company than products that are not accessible.

When accessibility features or capabilities have significant mainstream market appeal, and their incorporation will result in greater return on investment than would expending the same effort on something else, market forces alone can cause these features or capabilities to be incorporated into products and services. These instances should be identified and encouraged. Other accessibility features, however, no matter how low their cost, have not and will not occur in mainstream products without some induced effect on net profit. Regulations can be used to inject social values into the profit equation, but only if the regulations are enforced in a fashion that impacts profits positively if products are accessible, or negatively if they are not. "Pull" regulations (i.e., regulations that create markets and reward accessibility) generally work better than "push" regulations (i.e., regulations requiring conformance with regulatory standards), but both have a place in the development of public policies that bring about access and full inclusion for people with disabilities. Neither type of regulation works if it is not enforced. Enforcement provides a level playing field and a reward, rather than a lost opportunity, for those companies that work to make their products accessible. For enforcement to work, there must be accessibility standards that are testable and products that are tested against them.

Issues for Action

Seven general action items are advanced and discussed to address these issues:

#1 - Maximize the effectiveness of assistive technologies and lower their cost – in order to maximize people's general abilities and independence. Key strategies: Foster results-oriented R & D all the way to commercial availability.

#2 - Maximize the accessibility of mainstream information and communication technology products, so that people with disabilities and seniors can use standard products as they encounter them. Key strategies: Increase funding for research, proof of concept, and commercial hardening of approaches to accessible design of mainstream products to advance understanding in this area; craft accessibility regulations so as to help employees build business cases.

#3 - Ensure that access to the Internet and other virtual environments is provided, as it has been to physical places of public accommodation.

#4 - Address new barriers to the accessibility of digital media caused by digital rights management (DRM), including when visual and audio rights are sold separately.

#5 - Base all policy regarding information and communication technology (ICT) accessibility on a realization of the importance of the business case. Where a solid business case cannot be built based on market forces alone, create accessibility regulations and effective enforcement mechanisms that provide a clear profit advantage to those who comply and a disadvantage to those who do not.

#6 – Create accessibility laws and regulations that are not technology specific, but are based on the functions of a device. Provide clear guidance as to what is sufficient to meet the standard, and allow requirements to index themselves to technologies, as they evolve, using baselines. To the extent possible, harmonize laws and regulations with those of other countries for products that are sold internationally.

#7 – Ensure that up-to-date information about accessible mainstream technology (AMT) and assistive technology (AT) is available to and being used by the public.

INTRODUCTION

Information and communication technologies are changing at an ever-increasing rate. What used to be multi-year product life cycles have now decreased in many instances to life cycles of less than a year. Previous accessibility strategies involving the development of adaptive technologies, or accessible versions of new technologies, are failing due to this rapid turnover.[1] This is exacerbated by the fact that it is not just products that turn over, but the underlying technologies as well. For example, analog cell phones were made accessible just as they were being replaced with digital cell phones. Now some digital phone formats (e.g., TDMA) are being phased out in favor of newer technologies.[2] This same technology churn, however, is also opening up new opportunities for better assistive technologies and more accessible mainstream technologies.

The National Council on Disability undertook this project to explore key trends in information and communication technology, highlight the potential opportunities and problems these trends present for people with disabilities, and suggest some strategies to maximize opportunities and avoid potential problems and barriers. Many of the changes in technology are evolutionary, but some revolutionary changes are also ahead. Several of these changes may even cause a rethinking of concepts and the definitions of such terms as "disability," "assistive technology," and "universal design," or how these terms are used.

Several technology trends discussed in this paper present opportunities for universally designed products, and for improved availability, usability, and affordability of assistive technology that can have significant impact on the quality of life for individuals with disabilities. the more reliant society becomes on technology to perform fundamental aspects of every-day living, how we work, communicate, learn, shop, and interact with our environment , however, the more imperative it is that individuals with disabilities have access to that same technology, and the more costly will be the consequences of failure to ensure access. As the rate at which technology evolves increases exponentially, so does the potential for an unbridgeable technology divide.

The policies we adopt today will determine whether the technology of the future empowers individuals with disabilities, enabling them to work, learn, communicate, shop, and live independent, productive lives as full and equal members of society.

Technological Advances That Are Changing the Rules

In order to understand how technological advances can lead to the need to re-think technology and disability funding and policy, it is important to understand just how fundamentally things are changing. Four key technology trends have been selected for discussion in this report. Opportunities and barriers created by these advances follow in the next sections.

Some things in the discussion below challenge the imagination. Yet, except where indicated otherwise, everything discussed is already commercially available or has been demonstrated by researchers. This section is based on a more comprehensive and periodically updated list, complete with references and links, which can be found at www.trace.wisc.edu/tech-overview.

Trend 1: Ever-Increasing Computational Power Plus Decreasing Size and Cost

Computational power is growing at an exponential rate. At the same time, the size of electronic components is shrinking, decreasing product size, power consumption, and cost. Raymond Kurzweil helped to make this growth real to those not used to dealing in exponentials, with the following: In 2000, $1,000 could buy a computer that had the computational power of an insect. By 2010, $1,000 will purchase the computational power of a mouse. By 2020, $1,000 will purchase the computational power of the human brain. By 2040, $1,000 will purchase the computational power of all the brains in the human race.[3] Kurzweil has also "projected 2029 as the year for having both the hardware and software to have computers that operate at human levels."[4]

Personal digital assistants have shrunk from the size of paperback books to credit card size, and now to a function that runs in the back of a cell phone.[5,6] Cell phones have shrunk from something just under the size and weight of a brick to cigarette-lighter size, most of which is occupied by the battery. Multiple Web servers can fit on a fingernail (sans power supply), and RJ45 (Internet) cable jacks are available that have Web servers built directly inside the jack.[7]

Researchers have created gears the diameter of a human hair,[8] motors that are a hundred times smaller than a human hair,[9] and are now exploring tiny cellular-scale mechanisms that would use flagella to move about in the blood stream.[10] The entire field of nanotechnology is taking off, supported by major federal funding.

Although very expensive technologies are needed to create these devices, the cost per device is dropping precipitously. Sensors that were once hand-assembled are now created en masse, and sometimes even created in a "printing-like" process.[11] The cost of computing drops by a factor of 10 approximately every 4-5 years. It is not uncommon to find children's video games that have more computing power than supercomputers of just 10-15 years prior. Scientists are now turning to light instead of wires in microchips to keep up with the speed.[12]

This trend towards more computational power, with decreased size and cost, can make possible improved and entirely new types of assistive technology. This trend is also providing capabilities in mainstream technologies that can enable them to more easily and effectively meet the needs of people with disabilities.

Trend 2: Technology Advances Enabling New Types of Interfaces

The human interface is one of the most important determinants of whether a technology product can be used by people with disabilities. Advances in interface technology are creating new opportunities for better assistive technologies, more accessible mainstream technologies, and entirely new concepts for controlling both.

Projected Interfaces

Using a projector and camera, companies have created products that can project anything from a keyboard to a full display and control panel onto a tabletop, a wall or any other flat surface. People can then touch the "buttons" in this image. The camera tracks movements, and the buttons or keys operate as if they really existed.[13] One device is pocket-sized, projects a keyboard onto the tabletop, and allows users to enter data into their PDA by typing on the image of the keyboard on the tabletop.[14, 15] Other projected interfaces use sound waves.[16]

Virtual Interfaces

Going one step further, researchers have demonstrated the ability to project an image which floats in space in front of a person. With this glasses or goggle-based system, only the user can see the image floating there.[17] Some systems project the image directly onto the retina.[18] A pocket controller or gesture recognition can be used to operate the controls that float along the display. Motion sensors can cause the displays to move with the user's head, or stay stationary.

Augmented Reality

Researchers are also using this ability to project images to overlay them with what a person is seeing in reality, to create an "augmented reality." One project envisions travelers who can move about in a city in a foreign country by wearing a pair of glasses that automatically recognizes all of the signs and translates them. Whenever foreign travelers look at a sign, they would see a translation of that sign (in their native language) projected over the top of the sign.[19] [20]

Virtual Reality

Research on ultra high resolution displays has a target of being able to display images that appear with the same fidelity as reality. Researchers look forward to the day when the resolution and costs drop to the point that entire walls can be "painted" with display technology, to allow them to serve as "windows," work spaces, art work, or entertainment, as the user desires. Introducing three-dimensional viewing and displays that work in 360 degrees, researchers have a goal of eventually creating walls or environments that are indistinguishable from reality.

Realistic imaging technologies are already being used in classrooms, primarily to teach science. The ability to virtually "shrink oneself" can be used to explore things that would otherwise not be visible or manipulable by humans. The ability to zoom out can provide more global perspectives. The ability to carry out virtual chemistry experiments can allow students to conduct the experiments that are most interesting or educational, rather than those that are the safest (from poisoning or explosion) or cheapest (not involving expensive chemicals or elements). Time can also be expanded or compressed as needed to facilitate perception, manipulations or learning.[21]

Hands-Free Operation and Voice Control

There are already hands-free telephones. New phase-array microphones have been developed that can pick up a single person's voice and cancel out surrounding sounds, allowing communication and voice control in noisy environments.[22] There are cameras that can self-adjust to track a user's face, allowing face-to-face communication for those who cannot reach out to adjust cameras.[23] Rudimentary speech recognition is available on a $3 chip,[24] and speech recognition within a limited topic domain is commonly used. IBM has a "superhuman speech recognition project," the goal of which is to create technology that can recognize speech better than humans can.[25]

Speech Output

The cost to build speech output into products has plummeted to the point where speech can be provided on almost anything. All of the common operating systems today have free speech synthesizers built into them or available for them. Hallmark has a series of greeting cards with speech output that, at $3.99, are just 50 cents more than paper, non-electronic cards. Recently a standard cell phone that had been on the market for a year received a software-only upgrade and became a talking cell phone, with not only digitized speech talking menus, but also with text-to-speech capability for short message service (SMS) messages. The phone, with all speech functionality, sold for $29 with a service contract.[26]

Natural Language Processing

The capability of technology to process human speech continues to evolve. Although full, open topic natural language processing is not yet available, natural language processing for constrained topics is being used on the telephone and soon may allow people to talk successfully to products.

Artificial Intelligent Agents

Websites are available that allow users to text chat with a virtual person, who will help them find information on the site.[27] Research on task modeling, artificial intelligence, and natural language are targeted toward creating agents users can interact with, helping them find information, operate controls, etc. Often the subject of science fiction, simple forms of intelligent agents are reaching the point in technology development of becoming a reality in the home.

Microprocessor Controlled User Interfaces

When products are controlled by microprocessor running programs as they are today, they can be programmed to operate in different ways at different times. The use of more powerful processors, with more memory, is resulting in the emergence of new devices that can be controlled in many different ways and can be changed to meet user preferences or needs.

Multi-Modal Communication

There is a rapid diversification taking place in the ways people can communicate. Video conferencing allows simultaneous text, visual, and voice communications. Chat and other text technologies are adding voice and video capabilities. In addition, the technology to cross-translate between modalities is maturing. The ability to have individuals talking on one end and reading on the other is already available using human agents in the network.[28] In the future, the ability to translate between sensory modalities may become common for all users.

Direct Control from the Brain

External electrodes in the form of a band or cap are available today as commercial products for elementary control directly from the brain.[29] Research involving electrode arrays which are both external and embedded in the brain have demonstrated the ability to interface directly with the brain to allow rudimentary control of computers, communicators, manipulators, and environmental controls.

Trend 3: Ability to be Connected Anywhere, Anytime – With Services on Demand

New advances will soon enable people to be connected to communication and information networks no matter where they are. People can leave caretakers and still be a button-press away. Everything in the environment will be connected, most often wirelessly, allowing people to think about communication, control, and "presence" in entirely new ways. Individuals who have trouble with wires and connectors will not need them. Network based services can provide assistance, on demand, to people wherever they are. These advances will create opportunities for whole new categories of assistive technology.

Wireless Electronics – Connected World

There are already wireless headsets, computer networks, music players, and sensors. New technologies, such as ZigBee, will allow for devices that are very small, wirelessly connected, and draw very little power.[30] Light switches, for example, could run off a small ten-year battery and have no wires coming to or from them. People would simply place a light switch on the wall where it was convenient, at a convenient height. Flipping the switch would control the lights as it does now. If someone else needed the light switch in a different place, they would simply move it by pulling it off the wall and replacing it where desired, or placing an additional switch wherever they liked, including on their wheelchair or lap tray.

High speed wireless networks are also evolving, and costs are dropping. No wires will be needed between televisions, video recorders, or anything else (except sometimes the wall, for power). A person in a power wheelchair could have an on-chair controller connected to everything in the house, and yet still be completely mobile.

Virtual Computers

Computers may disappear, and computing power will be available in the network. Wherever a person is, he or she will be able to use whatever display is convenient, e.g., on the wall or in a pocket, to access any information, carry out computing activities, view movies, listen to music, etc. Instead of making each product accessible, things would exist as services and capabilities, which could be accessed through a person's preferred interface.

Control of Everything from Controller of Choice

New universal remote console standards have been developed that would allow products to be controlled from other devices.[31] Products implementing these standards could be controlled from interfaces other than the ones on the product. A thermostat with a touchscreen interface, or a stove with flat buttons, for example, could be controlled from a cell phone via speech, or from a small portable Braille device.

Location Awareness

GPS (Global Positioning System) devices enable people to determine their position when outside, and are already small enough to fit into cell phones and large wristwatches. Other technologies, such as RFID (Radio Frequency Identification) and devices that send signals embedded in the light emitted from overhead light fixtures, are being explored to provide precise location information where GPS does not work.

Object Identification

Tiny chips can be embedded into almost anything to give it a digital signature. RFID chips are now small enough that they are being embedded inside money in Japan.

Assistance on Demand – Anywhere, Anytime

With the ability to be connected everywhere comes the ability to seek assistance at any time. A person who doesn't understand how to operate something can instantly involve a friend, colleague, or professional assistant who can see what he or she is looking at and help work through the problem. Someone who needs mobility assistance could travel independently, yet have someone available at the touch of a button. These assistants could help think something through, see how to get past an obstacle, listen for something, translate something, or provide any other type of assistance, and then "disappear" immediately.

Wearable Technology

Today there are jackets with built-in music players, with speakers and microphones in the collar.[32,33] There are keyboards that fold up, and circuitry that is woven into shirts and other clothing. There are now glasses and shoes with a built-in computer that can detect objects within close proximity through echo location and then send a vibrating warning signal to the wearer. The shoes also will use a GPS System to tell the wearer where they are and which direction they are going.

Implantable Technology

There are cochlear implants to provide hearing. Heart and brain pacemakers are common. Increasing miniaturization will allow all types of circuits to be embedded in humans. In addition, research is continuing not only on biocompatible materials, but also on biological "electronics."

Trend 4: Creation of Virtual Places, Service Providers, Products

Possibly one of the most revolutionary advances in information and communication technologies has been the development of the World Wide Web. Although the Internet had been around for a relatively long time by the 1990s, Web technologies allowed it to be approachable and usable by people in a way not previously possible. It has not only given people new ways of doing things, but has fostered the development of entirely new social, commercial, and educational concepts. It also has allowed for virtual "places" that exist only in cyberspace. This includes virtual environments, virtual stores, virtual community centers, and complete virtual communities. E-travel is allowing people to go places and see things that once were only possible through books or documentaries. Electronic re-creation can allow people to explore real places, as if they were there, and at their own speed. They could wander a famous museum, for example. The Web also provides an array of products and services that is unmatched in physical stores in most localities.

NEW OPPORTUNITIES

Advances in information and communication technology will provide a number of new opportunities for improvement in the daily lives of individuals with disabilities, including work, education, travel, entertainment, healthcare, and independent living. There is great potential for more accessible mainstream technology with less effort from industry. There is also great potential for better, cheaper, and more effective versions of existing assistive technology (AT), and entirely new types or classes of AT.

Opportunity 1: More Accessible Mainstream Products (Simpler, More Adaptable, More Mainstream Benefit)

Some of the changes that will result from mainstream product design are evolutionary continuations of current trends. Other changes will be revolutionary, changing the nature of mainstream technologies and their usability by people with different types of disabilities. Some examples:

Potential for more built-in accessibility

Almost everything today, including cell phones, alarm clocks, microwaves, ovens, washers, and thermostats, is being controlled by one or more microcomputers. Even small devices like TV remote controls have a microcontroller inside. Because most everything is and will increasingly be controlled by programs running on increasingly powerful microprocessors, it is now possible to design products that will follow different instructions and behave differently for different users. Many products can already be adjusted to accommodate disabilities. For example, cell phones have a large print setting. Computers can be adjusted to work for people who have tremors. People can now watch television programs with or without captions. The Automated Postal Centers at many post offices offer touchscreen or tactile buttons and voice output. The ability to create a much broader range of products for the home, workplace, or public that can adapt to meet users' needs is continually increasing, and the cost is dropping. For example, speech is no longer a significant cost factor and can be added with little or no hardware costs.

Products that are simpler to use

Although the trend today is toward products that are ever more complex, we are on the cusp of a revolution in human interface. The ability for *unrestricted* voice recognition and natural language processing will come further in the future, and the ability to use these in practical ways in limited domains (e.g., controlling household appliances) is already emerging. When it arrives, the ability to simply tell products what should be done (e.g., "cook this at 450 for an hour," or "record *Wild Kingdom*," or "wake me at 8:30") will be a tremendous advance for individuals with cognitive disabilities or people who, for any reason, are unable to effectively use knobs, buttons, and menus on products. The mass market appeal of such a capability is enough to drive this into the marketplace on its own as soon as it is ready. For individuals who cannot speak, text input or an aid with speech output could be used.

Interoperability: To reduce the need for built-in direct access

Direct access is the ability of a user to operate a product without the need for assistive technology. Building direct access into products is generally the most effective, least stigmatizing, most available, and least expensive method of providing access to people with some types of disabilities. For people with other types of disabilities, particularly those with multiple and severe disabilities, it is sometimes not practical to build direct access into mainstream products. The types of interfaces required, such as dynamic Braille displays, electrodes, sensors mounted on the wheelchair, etc., typically cannot be included as standard parts for mainstream products. For these people, the best approach may be to access mainstream products by controlling them with special AT interfaces via a standard interconnection/control method. This would require these users to have a special AT interface device.

The new and emerging wireless interconnectivity technologies and universal remote console standards discussed earlier will enable people needing a special interface to approach a device, link to it, and operate it from their own interface. This could include most any device in the home, work, or community, from a thermostat to office equipment. Universal remote controllers could include any of the current and future types of AT, including devices with Braille displays, sip and puff controls, natural language interfaces, or some day, even direct-brain interfaces. This type of connectivity in mainstream products also has the mass market application of enabling control of products with voice or intelligent agents.

Flexible "any-modality" communication

The trend toward multi-modal communication (voice, video, chat) all using the same device, can be a boon for individuals with sensory disabilities, especially individuals who are deaf, hard-of-hearing, deaf-blind, or speech-impaired. If "any-modality" communication can be implemented in mainstream technologies with the same ubiquity as captions are on televisions, individuals who are deaf or hard of hearing will be able to use almost any phone. People who are deaf can use text mode. Those who are deaf but can speak can use speech to talk, and then read the display on the phone for text coming back to them. People who are hard of hearing can listen, and have text displayed in parallel, or when they cannot understand. Individuals who sign can use sign language, and individuals with cognitive disabilities can use gestures and visual cues to facilitate communication. If the evolving translation capabilities are added, services in the network can change communication modality as needed. Communicating with someone at a distance may be easier than communicating face-to-face. Building these capabilities into mainstream technologies also may greatly assist in the adoption and use of these modalities by individuals who acquire disabilities as they age, by reducing the stigma that would ordinarily be associated with using *special* technologies.

Where these advances have demonstrable mainstream benefit, adoption will be easier and faster. And, like closed captioning, will gain universal acceptance and consumer demand. Only some accessibility features, however, will have enough mainstream benefit to be introduced and be maintained. For the rest, support and/or incentives must be provided.

Opportunity 2: Better (Cheaper, More Effective) AT and New Types of AT

Technology advances will result in the improvement of current assistive technologies and the introduction of entirely new types of AT. Some of these technologies are realizable today. Some will emerge in the future. But all should be considered when setting policy today – due to the very slow pace at which policy changes as compared to technology.

Cost, size, and power
The rapid advances being made every year in reducing the size and increasing the power of electronic devices is leading to smaller, less expensive, and more intelligent products. This provides for a greater opportunity to create assistive technologies that previously would have been too big or required too much power.

Inexpensive technologies
One concern regarding the use of personal technologies by people with cognitive disabilities is the risk that the products will be lost or stolen. With core functions being implemented as services on the network, and technology costs dropping precipitously, portable devices that could support cuing and other AT functions for those with cognitive disabilities will soon be so inexpensive that they can be easily replaced if lost. To reach these price points, however, the devices will have to be based on common mainstream devices. As speech and natural language-enabled technologies and intelligent agent software improve, mainstream products that could be used in these ways may be possible within the next decade.

Wearable technologies
The trend toward wearable technologies will obviate the need for people with disabilities to carry devices, leaving their hands free for other tasks. This will be particularly helpful for people who use canes, walkers, and service animals, and generally already have at least one hand in use. People who have

a cognitive disability that makes it difficult to remember such devices, and who might therefore leave them behind, will also benefit from wearable technologies. Network-based services can further reduce costs by putting the intelligence and memory in the network and allow a new device to pick up where the last one left off, without any need for reprogramming. Very sophisticated communication and health-monitoring technologies can now be worn on the wrist or woven into clothes, making them less likely to be left behind. The trend is toward less expensive products with more functions.

Translating and transforming AT

Information throughout the environment is presented at a wide range of levels of complexity, which can create difficulties for people with cognitive disabilities. As researchers master the ability to create technology that can translate between languages, including translation between more complex and simpler languages, they are developing many of the tools needed to translate between different levels of complexity and vocabularies within the same language. These language translation technologies could be adapted to translate between sign languages and spoken languages.

A potential for new intelligent AT

With rapidly shrinking technologies, it will not be long before it is possible to implant imaging devices into contact lenses, so that even individuals with good vision could have enhanced vision, automated or human-based cuing on demand, text that could be read aloud by looking at it, etc. Such capabilities could be a boon to individuals with language, learning, or cognitive disabilities. Already, there are cameras that will read text when it is photographed, and concept glasses with built-in cameras that perform face recognition of whomever a person looks at. With the use of heuristics with increasing computing power, it is also possible to begin thinking about assistive technologies that would take in a complex display of information (e.g., all of the text visible down the corridor at the shopping mall) and present it to a person in a coherent way.

Human augmentation

In addition to making the world more usable by people with disabilities, advances in technology can also help enhance the overall abilities of people with disabilities to better interact with the world as they encounter it. Cochlear implants have been available for some time, as have prosthetic limbs. Research is progressing on artificial retinas. Advances in electronic imaging, robotics, and computer processing promise advances in all of these areas, enhancing people's basic abilities to access the world as they encounter it.

These new imaging and processing technologies also open the door for providing individuals with new and different ways to mitigate their disability. For example, an artificial eye might be able to provide enough vision for basic mobility, but not enough to read 10-point type. The same artificial eye, however, could have a processor and optical character recognition capability built in that could read any text the person looked at. The text could be read, changed to speech, and transmitted to a tiny earpiece. The person could then see a piece of paper well enough to pick it up, use their residual vision to direct the "reading" of the text, and have the text read into their ear. Using network connectivity, they could also have it translated, enhanced, or explained if needed. Combining technologies that mimic human abilities and provide enhanced super-human function in a single implantable prosthesis raises new opportunities and potentials for restoring function that go beyond the ability to restore natural vision.

Technologies that allow the unimaginable

Individuals are already using direct-brain control for rudimentary communication and manipulation activities. However, this currently requires that the skull be opened up and electrode arrays inserted. In the future, with advanced signal processing, it may be possible to read the signals from outside of the skull. Or, tiny sensors smaller than a blood cell might be injected into the bloodstream. Under computer control, they would be directed to swim to the brain, where they would position themselves, forming a sensor net powered by body processes or radiated power. They would provide a map of brain activity and feed it to an external sensor worn on glasses or earpieces and connect to a network, enabling the user to control the environment, drive a wheelchair, communicate, look up information, etc. No surgery would be required, and a device could fail without disrupting the network.

Opportunity 3: Decrease Net Cost while Increasing Quality of Life

Although the cost of technologies is continually decreasing, the cost is not zero. Some assistive technologies may in fact be expensive. The cost for some types of specialized technology could run to $10,000 or more (much more if it needs to be surgically implanted). The cost for failing to make technology accessible to people with disabilities, however, can be even higher. The 2005 average cost of nursing home care, for example, was over $60,000 a year for a semi-private room.[34,35] That leaves quite a margin for technologies that would delay entry into a nursing home by even 6 months or that could allow a person to live in a semi-dependent living situation.

BARRIERS, CONCERNS, AND ISSUES

Rapidly advancing technologies provide a host of new opportunities. However, they raise a number of issues and concerns as well. If not addressed, technology advances can pose new barriers to people with disabilities, including loss of access to products they had access to before the advances in technology.

1) Technology Trends That Move away from Accessible Interfaces toward Inaccessible Interfaces

Many of the same technological advances that show great promise of improved accessibility also have the potential for making previously accessible products less accessible. The following are some emerging technology trends that are causing accessibility problems.

Increasing complexity of devices and user interfaces
Products continue to have new functions, capabilities and accompanying interface complexity added to them. A recent industry survey showed that the rate at which consumers are returning new products has been increasing, with the "No Defect Found" return rate running 50 percent to as high as 90 percent + (depending on product category).[36] These data are for mainstream customers, but the impact of increasing complexity of products on individuals with cognitive disabilities is even greater. As a result, people with cognitive disabilities, including many seniors with cognitive disabilities, are finding it increasingly difficult to find appliances or products they can operate.

The trend toward digital controls

One problem for people with severe visual disabilities is the use of touch screens, soft keys, and display-based interfaces. Instead of knobs or dials that have a fixed function, the functions of the knobs or buttons may change from one moment to the next. The current function controlled by the button is usually displayed on the screen near the control. The use of scrolling cursors on on-screen menus is increasing. Products are becoming more complex, requiring individuals to think in terms of hierarchical menus. This type of product interface also requires users to operate controls with one hand while they are watching the display, which is difficult for those with certain cognitive disabilities and those without good motor control. In addition, these types of products provide an absolute barrier to individuals who are blind. Many people who are blind, who have used their own home appliances independently, are suddenly losing the ability to use their stove, washer, or dryer, as old models have to be replaced, and the only products now available use digital displays instead of tactile controls.

Devices too small and closed to physically adapt

The move toward miniaturization and device consolidation is leading to devices that are increasingly difficult to handle and operate. For example, where once there were a few very small phones, now most phones are very small and are harder to pick up and operate. Even the remote controls on televisions and audio equipment are getting smaller. Some have buttons that are very close together or have flat, tactilely featureless surfaces. While some people may prefer small products, the problem arises when there is neither an alternate way to operate these products nor alternate versions of the products that can be handled and used more easily.

Closed/Locked systems

Problems also arise from closed systems that do not provide any alternate control mechanism. Increasingly, concern about security and/or digital rights management is resulting in products that are physically closed and have closed software. That is, the products cannot be opened, and no hardware or software can be added to them. E-book readers that do not allow access to the book text (so that it can be read by screen reading software) and that allow publishers to turn off the native text reading capabilities of the e-book readers is one example.[37] AT cannot read the text, and the e-books' built-in reading feature is purposely disabled by the book publisher. The result is that, for those who cannot see or read well enough to read the visual text, access (built-in or AT) is denied. Computers in libraries and other shared use locations are another example of a closed system barrier to access. The personal computer is ordinarily thought of as being open, but it is typically "locked down" in a library so that users are not able to add software, peripherals, etc. Systems that are closed must have built-in accessibility or provide some mechanism for access through an alternate interface. The same problem exists in university computer labs. Information Services departments that do not want any foreign software installed, or hardware attached to machines, because of the risk of virus or security breaches, are yet another common example.

The trend toward automated and self-service devices in public places

The trend toward replacing ticket agents, cashiers, information personnel, and salespersons with less expensive ticketing, vending, cash, and information kiosks will continue as such terminals become more intelligent. In some cases these information-transaction machines operate alongside their human counterparts. In other cases, humans are completely removed from the scene and replaced by such information-transaction machines. For obvious reasons these machines are designed so that users cannot modify them. Automatic, self-service technology must be designed with a wide range of disabilities in mind, or people with disabilities no longer will have access to these ticketing, vending, cash or information services. NCD's 2006 position paper, *Access to Airline Self-Service Kiosk Systems,* describes the current problems people with vision impairments are experiencing in air travel due to inaccessible self-service ticket kiosks.[38]

The trend away from face-to-face interaction

This trend takes two forms. The first is the replacement of information and support people with automation. Interactive voice response systems (IVRs), Internet help pages that replace product support, and the above-mentioned information and transaction machines are examples of the move away from face-to-face customer service. Such systems are usually designed for individuals who do not have disabilities, and do not accommodate the variations that people with disabilities present. Interactive voice response systems (IVRs), for example, often are not operable in text mode. And if the person who is deaf accesses them through a relay operator, the additional communication delays often cause the IVRs to time out. Inaccessible Web pages can cause a similar problem for individuals who must rely upon technical support available solely through this medium, with no way to contact a human being.

The move away from face-to-face interaction is not occurring solely in information services. Education, commerce, work, and even social interaction are moving to the Web and to computer-mediated telecommunication forms. Universities are offering increasing numbers of educational programs via the Internet. Companies allow or require people to work from their homes or remote offices. Even when people are on the same campus, interactions and some types of work activities may be available only via computers and intranets. Some stores have been closed and moved to the Web. Some stores and businesses exist only on the Web.

The fact that all of these activities are now computer mediated can potentially be a great benefit to individuals who have disabilities. Computer mediation of the information and interactions makes it easier to translate the information into forms that people with sensory or learning disabilities can use. Such systems can also be far more usable by those with mobility impairments. However, if these systems and services are not accessible, many important aspects of society, such as education, work, and activities of daily living, will become inaccessible. Moreover, as things such as technical support and certain products and services become available exclusively via the Internet, they become unavailable to those unable to access those websites.

2) Technology Advancing into Forms Not Compatible with Assistive Technology

The second major concern is that the incorporation of some new technologies into products is causing the products to advance and change so fast that current accessibility techniques and strategies cannot keep pace. The rapid churn of mainstream technologies is faster than assistive technology development, and even mainstream technologies that are inherently accessible to a particular group can quickly churn out of the marketplace. To complicate the situation further, the convergence of functions is being accompanied by a divergence of implementation. The same functions are being implemented on different products using different technologies and/or standards, and interoperability between AT and mainstream technology exists only in a few areas and is not strong even there. Thus, the gap between the mainstream technology products being introduced and the availability of assistive technologies necessary to make them accessible will be increasing, as will the number of technologies for which no accessibility adaptations are available.

Convergence of function, but divergence of implementation

Much is said about the convergence of technologies, such as the melding of IT and telecommunications functions into a single device. However, a seldom-discussed issue is that the technologies, and standards used to implement them, are diverging. Different industries are creating converged technologies, but each is implementing them in different, and not always compatible, ways. For example, telephony, music, messaging, and television used to be four separate industries, each with its own technologies. Now all four industries are morphing into the others – but using different technologies to do so. Cellular telephones began with voice, and then text messaging was added. The ability to play music and share pictures came next. And now, with phones, users can download and watch television programs or pick up broadcasts.

Instant message software began with text messaging, and then voice was added, using a different technology than in cell phones or in VoIP phones. Video was then added, again using a different standard. New functions continue to be added.

Music players originally played only music, but now, using a variety of formats, they have branched into downloading and playing television programs. Voice communication is soon to follow, although it will probably use existing cell phone standards or perhaps VoIP. Messaging will likely accompany voice communication, using one of the several incompatible text protocols.

Internet Protocol Television (IPTV) began as simply Internet-based television. However, it, too, is rapidly expanding into music and telecommunications. If one is developing technologies on the Internet for broadcasting voice and video, why not also do point-to-point voice and video, or video phone calls? This is currently being developed within the IPTV structure – using yet another, different set of technologies and standards.

Even though what stands out at first glance is the convergence of functions into single devices, a more careful look reveals the divergence. For example, different methods, technologies and standards are being developed for voice communication. The result is an ever-increasing variety of technologies being used for voice, video, text, music, and delivery of television programs. However, few of these interoperate, and often the only common point they have is that the voice call function will work with the PSTN (public switched telephone network). Even within each of these domains there are competing standards. Those forms that are critical for mainstream use (voice, and perhaps video) will interoperate due to market pressures (i.e., any voice networks that are formed will interoperate because hearing people insist on being able to call each other). However, individuals who are deaf do not have the same degree of market clout, and have fewer choices about how they communicate with others. They may even be limited to communications only with others who have the same type of technology, or even the same device. Accessibility provisions designed for one medium (text communication on phones, captions on television) may be different or not extend to the same functions on other technology.

Lack of interoperability

The ability to patch mainstream technology (with modifications or AT) is limited both by the very fast churn rate and the increasingly closed nature of mainstream technology. Two strategies for access should therefore be increasingly relied upon: built-in accessibility and built-in interoperability. If mechanisms that allow the substitution of other interfaces are provided, systems that are otherwise "closed" can still be "open" for accessibility. For example, products with USB connectors that can be used to connect generic USB "human interface devices" (HID) interfaces, such as keyboards and mice, allow users to easily substitute alternative keyboards or mice. Moreover, these USB interface devices work across hardware and operating systems. For anyone who needs more interface modification than this, however, interoperability standards are non-existent, weak, or not supported. Several interoperability standards efforts have been launched but have faded and disappeared. One new interoperability standard is the universal remote console (URC) framework, which has been adopted as a family of ANSI standards (ANSI/INCITS 389-2005 through 393-2005) and is currently being developed as an ISO standard (ISO 24752). The standard allows for the operation of electronic products (even "closed" products) via other devices, which can present an alternate, accessible interface. However, concern by companies over product identity (the interface is what the person sees every day and develops a loyalty to) may hamper the adoption of such "alternative interface" standards in mainstream products.

Delay in accessibility when new technologies are announced

The lack of any systematic accessibility guidelines creates problems whenever any new technology is announced. Guidelines that are technology-specific will not be applicable to new technologies. Some recent examples:

CAPTCHA – When SPAM first started invading computer systems, CAPTCHAs were developed to help distinguish the software visitors from real visitors. Unfortunately, the initial and most common form was a visual character identification task that inadvertently prevented individuals who are blind from accessing any site that is protected by them. Only much later were alternatives developed.

DVD Menus – DVDs may contain movies with audio descriptions. However, audible access to the menus must also be provided in order for a user to take advantage of the audio description. Currently, for most DVDs, the user must have vision to be able to select the audio description from the menu.

CITRIX – This was an NT terminal service that allowed people to run software on thin client workstations. Used in the workplace, it lowered costs but provided no access for screen reader users, since all images and text on the screen were bitmapped images.

Cell Phones – These have quickly evolved from simple phones to devices with extensive menu-based functions. However, if people who are blind have no access to the menus, they cannot tell when they are making a free call or roaming at $1 a minute, and are unable to determine the battery charge or signal strength. The phones have had all of the hardware necessary for voice output, but it was not implemented, even as an option, until a complaint was filed with the FCC. The software was then changed in a phone that had already been on the market for over a year and the same phone with talking menus and text-to-speech reading of messages became available for $29.95 if a service plan was also being purchased.[39]

Hearing Aid Compatibility and Cell Phones – When the Hearing Aid Compatibility Act of 1988 was passed, an exception was made for cell phones because they were little used at the time. As digital phones were introduced they created severe interference for hearing aid users. Because of the 1988 exception, industry did not do anything to make these phones compatible during the initial stage of design. Although some research was conducted after consumers filed an FCC petition in 1995 to require hearing aid compatibility, the lack of progress on this issue over the next five years prompted consumers to return to the FCC in 2000 with urgent pleas for corrective action. Progress on compatibility did not begin until 2003, long after the introduction of digital phones, when the FCC approved a schedule by which certain percentages of wireless phones would have to be hearing aid compatible. By this time 88 percent of all wireless telephone subscribers used digital services.

History Repeated

As we move forward, the same pattern is being repeated. New technologies, without accessibility, are being introduced. Only when their use becomes widespread do we require accessibility. However, by then, retrofitting accessibility is more complicated, more expensive (sometimes *much* more expensive), and often less effective than if accessibility had been included in the original design and specifications.

The same pattern is being repeated in digital homes, biometrics, e-government, VoIP, digital rights management (DRM) in digital media, Web 2.0, Next Generation Network (NGN), and digital television (beyond captions and audio descriptions).

3) Technology Advancing into Forms Not Covered by Accessibility Rules

Another barrier is created when a type of product is covered under accessibility laws, but the product or product function evolves into a new technology and accessibility provisions no longer apply or are no longer effective. Some examples of the ways this can happen are:

Technology changing faster than regulations that govern it

Current legislative and regulatory framework is structured around particular types of technology. Rules apply to the built environment, transportation, telecommunications, and information technology. It is now becoming clear that the lines between these technologies are blurring. If two people make a phone call using the phone in their kitchen, and one is connected to the PSTN while the other is connected via the Internet, is it a phone call? High speed broadband Internet services were ruled by the FCC to be information services and generally not covered under telecommunications laws.

Recently, the FCC ruled that interconnected VoIP services (i.e., those that connect to the PSTN), must comply with certain telecommunications regulations, including those requiring emergency call handling and the submission of one's facilities to electronic surveillance. Most of the remaining telecommunications requirements, including those requiring accessibility, however, have not been applied to these new technologies, because the FCC has determined that VoIP is not a telecommunication service. People who switched from their local provider to their cable provider for phone service, using the same phones in their houses, suddenly were no longer covered by the telecommunications accessibility standards and protections. In the future, when people call family or colleagues using IPTV, and share with them video documents while they talk with them, will this be television, telecommunications, or information technology?

If classrooms with built-in tele-collaboration walls allow the class to take place in multiple locations, thus allowing better educational opportunities in rural areas, is this access to a built environment, information technology, or telecommunications?

Currently, there are gaps in our laws that require only certain things in certain environments to be accessible. These gaps will increase as new product types are developed. In addition, the shifting of functions into different technology types, such as phone calls now being made over the Internet and soon to be made using television sets, rather than just using the PSTN, will result in functions once protected by accessibility regulations, that are no longer protected. A model based on function versus technology and a model that is uniform across technologies is needed. For example, instead of regulations that apply only to telephones, access regulations should apply to any technology used for telecommunications.

Access requirements tied to technologies that become obsolete, with no requirements for access to new forms of technology

TTYs and captioning are two primary examples. The purpose of the TTY is to allow individuals who are deaf to communicate in text over phone networks. In IP networks, the TTY often doesn't work, and other IP text standards have been developed. However, without a requirement for text conversation technologies in IP-based voice telephony (VoIP), deaf people may be excluded from this communication modality as the world shifts from PSTN to VoIP. Perpetuation of the technology-specific TTY (Baudot code) will not serve them, because of connection, transport, and other problems. What is needed is a generic requirement for a reliable real-time text conversation capability wherever there is voice. This can then be combined with a requirement to interoperate with legacy PSTN text formats and with text in other interconnected voice and text conversation technologies. This would provide a requirement for the function desired without tying it to past technologies. Similarly, captions are currently encoded within the TV signal. However, that part of the signal would not exist on IPTV or when TV shows are downloaded or streamed from the Internet, so those regulations are ineffective. Restricting captioning requirements to one or a few particular transmission format(s) will result in growing gaps and for some - no coverage.

Funding for old paradigms implemented in new ways

Accessibility challenges can arise when there is a loss of funding for previously covered services as new technologies are utilized. For example, reimbursement for telemedicine can be problematic. Telemedicine holds great potential for individuals with mobility disabilities – particularly in rural areas. However, third party payers are not reimbursing for telemedicine services the same as for in-person medical services.

Another example is artificial personal assistants. As artificial personal assistants become real, effective, and cost-effective, will they be reimbursable? If people can live more independent, less expensive, and more productive lives with occasional tele-coaching or security monitoring, would artificial assistants be covered by private insurers or Medicare and Medicaid? Or would assistance and mentoring services not be reimbursed unless the person moves into a nursing home?

Another constraint can arise when funding for mainstream technologies is used to meet an AT need. If mainstream technologies can be repurposed to meet the needs of a person who has a disability better than purpose-built assistive technologies, will they be reimbursable to the same extent and in the same manner as purpose-built assistive technologies?

Open vs. content-constrained Internet connections

There is currently much debate about whether those who provide Internet connections to a house, or other location, should be able to control the types of information sent to the house, by whom, and at what level of quality connection. What if those who provide the connection are allowed to decide who will be able to provide information to the house (e.g., video and telephony) or are allowed to limit high performance connection to specific suppliers? If, for a given household, the access or performance preference is determined by the Internet provider to be Company A, and a person in that household who has a disability needs products from Company B (because Company B carries the accessible product), the person could be prevented from obtaining the Company B product by the Internet provider's policy. Similarly, if the person needs to use an alternate technology provided by Company C, he or she may find its performance is degraded, causing accessibility problems or even blocked access. This problem is exacerbated by the fact that individuals may have to use their technologies from multiple locations and not just from their homes. Absent consumer choice, a person with a disability may not be able to call from any house but their own. Unless the Internet operates more like the public road system, where individuals are allowed to take any vehicle that meets safety standards onto the road, rather than having to drive only certain companies' vehicles on certain roads or to certain locations, individuals who must rely on accessible versions of technologies will run into problems.

Digital rights management (DRM)

A very interesting sub-area in this discussion is digital rights management. While the need to protect the rights of those who publish things is critical, the ability to allow access for people with disabilities must be addressed as well. If content is to be locked so that it cannot be copied electronically, then some mechanism for rendering it in different forms should be built into the secure digital media players. For example, if a digital book can be presented visually but the text can not be read by the operating system (so that assistive technology such as screen readers could read it aloud), then a mechanism within the book player for enlarging it and reading it aloud should be provided. Technologically, this is not a problem, and voice synthesizers with speed control can be, and have been, built into the e-Book products directly. A marketing policy, however, whereby publishing companies sell the print (visual access) rights for a book to one distributor but the audio (spoken) rights for the book to another, has created an obstacle. Book player companies have been required to support a bit in their players that, when set by a book publisher, will prevent the voice output option in the book player from functioning. Thus, even though the book reader is capable of reading the book to the blind person, it will not perform that function if the book publisher sets the bit that tells the book reader to not read this book aloud. The same book is also protected so that it cannot be read by any other technology.

Interestingly, advances in optical character recognition and imaging technologies may cause a shift in digital rights management. However, if audio access is tied to marketing preferences, then the problem is likely to persist and must be addressed. This will be especially important with the rapidly aging population that has increasing difficulty seeing print media.

Assistive technologies that exceed human abilities

It is well known that although wheelchair users have trouble with stairs and other obstacles, they out-perform people who are walking on smooth surfaces. For example, in the Boston Marathon the women's wheelchair champion (1:43:42) was 20 percent faster than the men's running champion (2:07:14). And people who use power chairs and, sometimes, manual chairs, must travel more slowly when walking with someone who is on foot. We wouldn't think of only funding wheelchairs that went as fast as people walk, but funding limitations have been placed on the purchase of some communication and writing aids that went beyond basic speech or writing capabilities. For example, there have been cases in which a device that only provided speech output was reimbursable, but a general purpose laptop that was cheaper, and that also provided speech output was not reimbursable. How will this be dealt with when we get to human augmentation, artificial vision, etc.? Like the wheelchair, these technologies are likely to be inferior in some respects but superior in others. Will they be considered assistive technology or performance enhancement? In competitions, the answer is clearer, but, as we have seen with the ADA case involving whether a golfer with a mobility impairment could use a golf cart during competitions,[40]still tricky. The broader question will come with the provision of assistive technologies for activities of daily living, education, and work. If the devices restore function up to the level of that of people without disabilities, there would likely be no problem. But what if in providing devices to offset disability, the device gave super-human ability? Would this be covered by rehabilitation programs, government programs or insurance? What if someone with a disability wanted an enhancement in another ability, in order to be more employable? If this could be accomplished via training, would it be covered? Would it be covered if it were augmentation? How is it different? Why is it different? Should it be covered?

4) Definitions of Disability, Assistive Technology, and Universal Design

Rapidly evolving technologies might cause a rethinking of the definitions of disability, assistive technology, and universal design. At a minimum, they may change the way these words are used and how they are interpreted in legislation, regulation, and eligibility policy.

Definition of Disability

If a person is blind and gets an artificial retina/eye, is he or she no longer blind? Does it depend on quality of vision achieved? Would one qualify for training with the new eye if he or she can see fine but doesn't know how to interpret what is seen? Does the person qualify for accommodation? Other services? Can the person drive? Will new eye tests for driving be required? What if the eye fails a year later? Does the person qualify for a new eye? Or does the person have to wait for some period of months or years in a "blind" condition before again being classified as "disabled?"

A person may, in the future, be outfitted with a cybernetic eye, enabling the person to see general shapes for walking, to zoom in with image stabilization to read letters, and to employ OCR to read text. Assuming the person can now pass current eye tests and read any text, is the person blind? Can the person drive? Does the person qualify as blind? If the person qualified for government or insurance funding for the original cybernetic eye, and is now no longer "disabled" will the person qualify for an upgrade or replacement when it fails?

Definition of Assistive Technology (AT)

Currently, there are many definitions for "assistive technology." Some definitions focus on products that are purpose-built for people with disabilities. Other definitions refer to any technologies, including mainstream technologies that are used by a person with a disability to help offset the disability.

The definition is not always important, but may be in the case of deciding whether funding, tax breaks, or accommodations apply. Is an accessible mainstream product considered to be AT for this purpose? Is a feature in a mainstream product that makes things accessible considered to be AT or universal design (UD)? If there were an AT deduction for people who must buy AT to offset their disability, would mainstream technology that is accessible qualify? Some of it? All of it? None of it? If not and it does the same thing as an AT product would – why not?

Universal Design / Accessible Mainstream Technologies

Universal design is usually defined as a process, not as a thing or outcome. Universal design is the process of creating products that are usable by as wide a range of people as is commercially possible.

There is telecommunication legislation that requires products to be accessible when doing so is "readily achievable." When doing so is not "readily achievable," the legislation requires that products be compatible with assistive technology if that is "readily achievable." So when is something directly accessible vs. accessible via AT?

Cell phones today have features such as ring-tones or special capabilities, such as GPS navigation, that can be selected and activated from a menu on the phone. Sometimes these features are already in the phone. Sometimes they are downloaded into the phone only when selected. Sometimes the user gets the feature for free (if included in the price of the phone and service). Sometimes the user pays for the features. Sometimes the feature is provided by the phone or service provider. Sometimes it is provided by a third party.

Now let's assume that the feature in question is an accessibility feature.

- If it is in the phone – is it an accessible product ("built-in" accessibility)?
- If it is downloaded – is it built-in or AT?
- If the user can't tell that it is downloaded and it is free – isn't it "built-in" for all intents and purposes?
- If the user has to pay for it – isn't it then AT? No matter who provides it? (It is an add-on that must be purchased separately to make the phone accessible.)
- What if other people also have use of it – but have to pay for it? Would people with disabilities also have to pay for it? Is it AT then? Is it just another product that happens to be accessible? Is that true even if it is only a convenience for others but it is the only way that a user with a disability can use the phone?

If these questions are examined carefully, one can see that the same feature on the same product might be considered AT or accessible design depending on who uses it, how they use it, and who has to pay for it.

Why do we Care?

Definitions are academic unless they are used to legislate, to regulate, or to fund. Unfortunately, all of the above terms are used in all of these ways (e.g., program eligibility, funding, tax breaks, etc.).

No ready solution presents itself for this problem except perhaps to move away from a model that focuses on types of devices and categorization and toward a model based on function and the role of devices.

Part of the solution may be achieved by defining terms in a way that is specific to the context rather than expecting a "one definition fits all" approach for each concept.

5) Central Role of the Business Case

Finally, there should be a broader recognition of the importance of the "business case." This report focuses on new technologies and how they can benefit people with disabilities. None of these technologies will benefit anyone unless they are built into products, made available, and supported. And none of that will occur in any reliable or sustained fashion unless individuals within companies can make a business case for each feature.

Net profit is the primary reason products make it to the marketplace and remain on the market, and the primary reason ideas carry forward from one version of a product to other products. This is not specific to disability issues. It is true of every aspect of every product. It is often remarked that the problem is that companies care about nothing but profit— usually with a negative connotation. It is important to note that almost all of the companies involved in information and communication technologies are publicly traded companies, and the "owners who care about nothing but profit" are the public stockholders. Those who own stocks or have pensions usually ask nothing of their stock or pension managers except that they maximize return (profit, pension value, etc.). Environmental and sweatshop issues may sometimes impact shareholders' decisions, but there are no stakeholder directives to companies to "make accessible products" or "do good things for people who have disabilities." Profit, therefore, should be viewed in the same way one views gravity. It is neither good nor bad. It simply is. It is a force, and a very critical force, that drives industry and makes our economy work.

If a goal of our society is to have products that are accessible to and usable by people with disabilities, then some way must be found to make products that exhibit these characteristics generate significantly more net revenue for a company than products that do not. Business cases come from significant market demand or significant, enforced regulation – both of which affect the bottom line or net profit.

In some cases, more accessible and usable products will have a large enough market to generate their own business case. Where the technologies or techniques can be demonstrated to industry and shown to be more profitable than other design options or investments, the features or capabilities will become available through natural market forces. For a large portion of the population with disabilities, however, natural market forces have not and will not result in accessibility features in mainstream products over time.[41] [42]

Regulation is society's way of injecting social value into the business equation.[43] [44] Regulations can make it more profitable to create accessible products by rewarding accessibility with sales. No regulations are effective, however, without enforcement. Without enforcement there is no economic incentive to follow accessibility guidelines. In fact, there is a disincentive because companies that focus on accessibility worry that, while they are spending time and effort on accessibility, their competitors are spending their resources on other activities.[45] Enforcement of accessibility regulations has the effect of leveling the playing field. Companies that invest in accessibility know that their competitors must also be focusing on accessibility. Laws and regulations such as Section 508, when enforced, provide a competitive advantage to those who have more accessible products.

Section 508 has had a decided and positive, if somewhat limited effect on accessibility of electronic and information technology (E&IT) and on the willingness of E&IT companies to work with assistive technology vendors. However, the lack of enforcement of Section 508, the inability of purchasing agents to be able to judge the relative accessibility of the various products in the market, and the lack of any certification of compliance by companies have greatly reduced the potential impact of Section 508. The current voluntary product accessibility template (VPAT) does not provide a reliable way to determine conformance to 508, since purchasing agents cannot tell the difference between a VPAT that has been filled out with carefully considered information, and those that have not. Even when accurate, the VPAT only provides information that "relates" to each provision, but does not certify that the product meets any of the 508 provisions. This is left to the purchasing agents who do not have the time or the training to determine 508 compliance for each product type they procure. As a result, the primary enforcement agent (the purchasing agent) does not have the information necessary to know for certain if a product meets (fully or partially) any of the Section 508 provisions. Some mechanism for providing the purchasing agent with reliable assertions of conformance to the individualism provisions of 508 is needed for the Section 508 to be effective.

Regulations that are subject to strict enforcement and that have significant impact also result in better compliance. Regulations that are not enforced have little or no effect. In the electronic and information technology field, one can watch the efforts and teams in companies grow and shrink regularly in direct proportion to enforcement or perceived or anticipated enforcement.

To have more accessible information and communication technologies, we should provide the means for building a solid business case for those companies and employees who want to have more accessible products. Strong enforcement is one key element for this.

ISSUES FOR ACTION

There are many recommendations that could be made to minimize barriers and maximize opportunities inherent in the technology trends discussed above. Most can be found in other reports on this topic from NCD and others, such as NCD's 2004 report, *Design for Inclusion: Creating a New Marketplace*[46] and *Within Our Reach: Findings and Recommendations of the National Task Force on Technology and Disability.*[47]
Seven key action items are highlighted here.

#1 - Maximize the effectiveness of assistive technologies and lower their cost – in order to maximize people's general abilities and independence. Key strategies: Foster results-oriented R & D all the way to commercial availability.

Advancing technologies provide an opportunity to improve existing assistive technologies and to create entirely new types of AT not previously possible. Where these assistive technologies can restore function and allow individuals to work or live independently, or live more independently longer, the benefits and cost savings both to the individual and to society can be very significant. With a rapidly aging society, improving access to technology is becoming increasingly important. Providing access is shifting from a social issue to an economic issue.

- An inexpensive hand-held text reader could be developed using the same technologies that are rapidly shrinking in cost and size. About the size of a candy bar, the text reader could be held or waved over any text that then would be read to the user in a logical fashion. A pill bottle could be scanned, enabling individuals with low vision to confirm the dosage and check that the medication is for them. Any printed text could be made accessible.
- Advanced GPS combined with RFID tags in the environment could be used by anyone wanting better navigation, even inside buildings. GPS can be found in cell phones that sell for $69 with phone plans. One can envision a cell phone that could be programmed to guide anyone, including those with vision or cognitive disabilities, directly to the door of an office.
- Many individuals who are deaf communicate primarily in sign language, which has syntax quite different from English syntax. As a

result, the written text of some deaf people can have grammatical mistakes much different than those of native English speakers. Grammar-checking software checks for common grammar errors made by people who speak. Development of a tool that will correct the written grammar of individuals who rely on sign language as their primary mode of communication would be a great educational aid, improve their written communication, and open up conversation with non-signing speakers.

- Practical devices to enhance the functioning of a person's language, learning, and cognitive disabilities have been limited to date. However, the sheer processing power that will soon be available, together with the ability to always be connected, and the shrinking size of devices, may make possible completely new approaches to providing assistance in this area.

- When the FCC asked for comments on its proposal to provide additional spectrum for use by new medical devices, it noted: "Implanted or body-worn devices in the future could enable paralyzed individuals to control artificial limbs by thought, through wireless interfaces between brain, nerve and muscle. The vision-impaired might have some degree of visual ability restored with the help of a microchip placed in the back of the eye. Even today, implanted vagus nerve stimulators that send electric pulses to the brain are being used to treat severe chronic depression. Tremors related to Parkinson's disease are being treated with deep brain stimulation implants. With other new types of implants, such as insulin pumps, physicians could wirelessly retrieve data and then make operating parameter adjustments with greater ease and accuracy than with the more traditional wired connection technologies, and in some cases, changes can be effected immediately by computer control. For health care providers and patients, such wireless implant monitoring technologies have the potential to lower medical costs by extending the time between hospital visits and surgical procedures."

Funding is needed to explore and develop emerging technologies that can be used to improve assistive technologies for people with disabilities.

Advances in AT make it possible for many more people to access the environment as they encounter it. This is particularly important for those with more severe or multiple disabilities, where creating accessible mainstream technology that addresses their needs is not always possible. Aids that can provide individuals with the ability to see, hear, read, navigate, and control things with their thoughts have all been demonstrated at least on a rudimentary level. Maximizing the abilities of people with disabilities will reduce the barriers encountered in the environment. This is particularly important for people with severe or multiple disabilities since building direct access into products for people with severe or multiple disabilities can often be a challenge.

#2 - Maximize the accessibility of mainstream information and communication technology products, so that people with disabilities and seniors can use standard products as they encounter them. Key strategies: Increase funding for research, proof of concept, and commercial hardening of approaches to accessible design of mainstream products to advance understanding in this area; craft accessibility regulations to help employees build business cases.

Although assistive technologies can enhance the abilities of some people to access and use the environment, the strategy of adapting individual mainstream technologies is limited to those technologies that are within an individual person's control. Even then the rapid rate of technology advancement is moving beyond the ability of AT to keep up in many or most areas. Far and away the most desirable situation would be for everyone to directly access and use mainstream technologies effectively and efficiently. People with disabilities and seniors want to use the same products that everyone else uses. They do not want to be limited to specialized products that are more costly and often, less functional. This isn't always possible, but it is the most economical mechanism for people who have limitations, and for society as a whole. In fact, given the aging population, this is not just a social imperative but an economic one as well. Additional funding is needed for research to develop better strategies for building accessibility into mainstream products and for quantifying when and where built-in accessibility can provide a significant return on investment.

Broad application and enforcement of existing accessibility standards, such as Section 255 of the Telecommunications Act of 1996 and Section 508 of the Rehabilitation Act of 1973, as amended, would result in the widespread adoption of universal design principles into the mainstream technology marketplace. This could be accomplished by lowering the hurdles to filing complaints, carrying out enforcement actions more quickly, and providing expert guidance and examples. The "sufficient techniques" approach discussed below is one way to provide such guidance and examples. One important step would be to move from a declaration to a certification model. That is, rather than companies simply stating what they have done to make their product accessible, without any warranty as to whether it meets the standards, companies would certify which accessibility provisions the product meets and which it does not. Purchasing agents and other customers are currently not able to evaluate whether products meet accessibility standards because different vendors now provide different types of information, using different terminology, to describe features on their products. They also use different standards for "meeting" a provision. As part of the design process, vendors should carefully evaluate their products against accessibility standards, and report which access provisions are met. This would make it much easier for purchasing agents to apply accessibility provisions in the purchasing process. Companies that can accurately evaluate the accessibility of their products should not be forced to use third-party certification services. As in many other areas, companies should be allowed to self-certify, provided they furnish supporting evidence and information sufficient to enable purchasers to know whether a product meets a particular access standard.

Purchasing requirements ("pull" regulations) seem to fit best with the business model. Expanding the use of Section 508-like purchase requirements into markets other than the Federal Government, could have a strong effect on the availability of mainstream products usable by people who have disabilities, including those who are seniors. Expanding beyond just E&IT is also important. Again, rather than mandating that all products manufactured must meet accessibility standards ("push" regulations), a better place to start might be with "pull" regulations, where products that are purchased for use in certain environments, such as for use by state and local governments, public schools, and entities that receive government financial assistance, would be required to meet accessibility regulations. This would motivate companies to add accessibility features to their products in order to better compete in these markets, but yet allows for the sale of products outside of these markets. A tipping effect can occur over time in a more natural fashion. This works better for mass market products where one product is manufactured and sold both to the government and to the public. It does not work as well for services or products that are built individually for different customers. It also does not work as well for products not used by governments, public schools, or by entities receiving government financial assistance. "Push" regulations would be required for markets not reached by "pull" regulations, or when "pull" regulations do not prove to be effective.

#3 - Ensure that access to the Internet and other virtual environments is provided, as it has been to physical places of public accommodation.

Because the Web as we know it did not exist when accessibility laws were written, this important area was not specifically mentioned in accessibility laws. Yet the world is changing rapidly and more and more education, socializing, daily living, commerce and employment are being carried out using network-based services. Some stores already appear exclusively on the Internet. Many specialty shops have disappeared altogether, especially in smaller communities. The only way to secure some types of products or services is over the Internet. Employees work remotely, connecting through the Internet. Colleges teach some courses in this fashion. Many other courses assume or require that students access information or carry out exercises via the Internet.

Since these virtual environments did not exist at the time the original accessibility laws such as the ADA were written, these technologies and environments were not mentioned specifically in the Act. NCD analyzed the issue of the ADA's applicability to the internet in its 2003 publication *Application of the ADA to the Internet and the Worldwide Web*,[48] and concluded that the ADA does apply to the internet.

Courts have not been consistent in their approach to this issue, however, and individuals with disabilities have had to resort to litigation for resolution of the matter. Some companies that have been sued for inaccessible websites argue that since these virtual environments did not exist at the time the original accessibility laws such as the ADA were written, the intent was to cover businesses' physical facilities only, not their websites. One such suit is pending in the Ninth Circuit.[49] The Internet and other virtual environments that exist, or may evolve, such as intranets and other networks and virtual environments, are becoming central to almost every activity in life and a powerful tool in enabling individuals with disabilities to live productively and independently.

#4 - Address new barriers to the accessibility of digital media caused by digital rights management (DRM), including when visual and audio rights are sold separately.

We are moving toward digital publication of most of our information. This has great potential for increasing the accessibility of information through flexibility of presentation. However, the combination of digital rights management (an important reality), marketing practices, such as selling visual and audio rights separately, and the lack of built-in accessibility is causing severe access barriers. Mechanisms and/or legislative changes are needed to address these new barriers. Opening up media to allow it to be electronically read may introduce piracy issues; thus, requirements for access to be built into players may be necessary. However, allowing individuals who have disabilities to legally and effectively access digital media using their own tools would be more effective for some, especially individuals who are deaf, blind, or deaf and blind, where including access features like a Braille display into every player may not be practical. Working with vendors of mainstream DRM devices to allow access via those special assistive technologies may be a solution. The issue of publishers blocking access by permanently turning off built-in accessibility features (example: "reading aloud" features) on a book-by-book basis must also be addressed.

#5 - Base all policy regarding information and communication technology (ICT) accessibility on a realization of the importance of the business case. Where a solid business case cannot be built based on market forces alone, create accessibility regulations and effective enforcement mechanisms that provide a clear profit advantage to those who comply and a disadvantage to those who do not.

Encourage companies to build access into their products by highlighting instances in which accessible products lead to profit. Where it is not clear that accessibility will lead to profit, however, a different mechanism should be used to enable people within companies who want to make their products more accessible to build a business case for doing so. For features and products lacking a natural business case, society must create regulations and enforcement mechanisms that impact profit and provide profit advantage to those who comply and disadvantage to those who do not. Creating conformance assertion mechanisms to make it clear when and where a product has met individual regulatory provisions will be key to compliance.

#6 - Create accessibility laws and regulations that are not technology specific, but are based on the functions of a device. Provide clear guidance as to what is sufficient to meet the standard, and allow requirements to index themselves to technologies, as they evolve, using baselines. To the extent possible, harmonize laws and regulations with those of other countries for products that are sold internationally.

Regulatory standards should be based on principles rather than technologies or product categories. In the past, different guidelines have been written for different technologies. One set of guidelines was developed for telecommunications, another for ATMs, another for information technologies, etc. Guidelines were also written differently for categories such as "open" and "closed" information systems.

These distinctions are blurring with modern technologies. Given any set of definitions it is possible to identify many products that fall into gray areas. There are also products that perform various functions, leading to a situation where one set of guidelines would apply to one function of a product, and another set would apply to another function.

Guidelines should be function and performance based, as well as technology neutral. Although this has a tendency to make guidelines more abstract, which can make them harder to understand and apply, two concepts that can help address this issue are "baselining" and "sufficiency."

Baselines

Technologies today are advancing so quickly that the standards and regulatory processes cannot keep up. In particular, regulations should be stable over time, yet technologies are constantly changing. The challenge is to create accessibility regulations, which make sense today, and that will work for technology of tomorrow. On the other hand, accessibility standards and regulations cannot be written with only the future in mind. It is not useful to write accessibility standards that will generate products that will be accessible someday, but will not work with the technologies that people with disabilities have today.

By introducing baselines, standards can be indexed to account for technology changes over time. Essentially, baselines are sets of technologies or features that it has been established are compatible with assistive technologies that consumers use. Products must then be accessible using technologies or features in the baseline. Over time, the technologies the users have can change, allowing for a natural progression without the need to rewrite standards. The approach is also more predictable and is function-based rather than based on a particular solution.

Sufficiency

A challenge in using more function-based standards is that they lack specificity. Functional standards allow innovation but can make it harder to determine if the standard has been met unless one is an expert in the area. Another problem is the tremendous variety of technologies. Although the essential requirements for accessibility may remain the same, the actual techniques to implement them can vary widely from technology to technology.

What works on a fare machine, may not work on a hand-held device. And what works on a personal workstation where software can be downloaded and installed, may not work on a shared public terminal, which cannot be modified by users.

With sufficiency, guidelines can be written in clear, testable form. Techniques which are "sufficient" at this point in time to meet the guidelines can then be established. As new techniques are created that are sufficient to meet the guidelines, they can be evaluated, documented, and added to the list of "sufficient" techniques without changing the guidelines. In this manner the list of techniques which are "sufficient" and the conditions under which they can be used can be periodically updated to reflect changing times and changing understandings without having to rewrite the fundamentals for accessibility.

Different sets of "sufficient" techniques could be identified for different categories of products. For example, techniques that involve the use of special technologies which might be installed on a product might be considered sufficient for a workstation, but would not be sufficient on a public information terminal where users are not allowed to install their own adaptive software. Using a "product line" approach may be sufficient if users are presented with the entire product line at the time of purchase, but not if they are only presented with a subset of the product line (not including the accessible versions) when they shop, nor would it be sufficient if these models were not included in special deals, or available as part of bundles. The use of "sufficient" techniques would not add or subtract from the guidelines, but can make it very clear to purchasing agents, manufacturers, and others, which techniques do or do not meet the guidelines, without the purchasing agents, manufacturers, and others having to be experts in the field.

The use of baselines and sufficiency can also foster the development of specific technologies, that, once available, can allow much more flexible techniques to be sufficient. For example, if new techniques for Web access are developed and incorporated into assistive technologies that could handle new Web technologies it would no longer be necessary to provide accessible alternatives to content presented using those technologies. That technology could then be added to the baseline. When and where all text phones can handle a new IPText format, (and all TTY text that remains is translated into the new IPText format) then IPText support alone could be sufficient. This approach can also facilitate international harmonization where different levels of AT may exist for different languages or cultures.

If done properly, even the questions of open and closed technologies can be addressed in a way that minimizes gray areas, and when gray areas are encountered, the impact on the consumers of a decision either way would be minimal. That is, in those "gray" cases where it becomes unclear whether A or B situation applies, either one would lead to a reasonable accessibility outcome and could be chosen.

Need for harmonization

Key to the effectiveness of any accessibility standards and regulations in this global economy is harmonization. It is difficult for companies that develop a product for multiple countries to create a single product line that addresses conflicting regulatory standards. The key word here is "conflicting." Standards can be different and still be harmonized. For example, one standard could ask for noise to be 15 decibels down from the signal and another could ask for it to be 20 decibels down. These two are harmonized, because creating products 20 decibels down would meet both standards. Harmonization does not mean that the standards must be the same, only that they must not conflict. It must be possible to meet all of the standards at the same time. But it is not necessary for all countries to have the exact same standards or regulations. Requiring that all standards or regulations be identical would be unfair to developed countries (holding them back) as well as developing countries (forcing them to adopt standards they might not be able to meet). However, it should be possible to design products that are marketed and sold in identical form internationally in a way that would fall within the accessibility standards or regulations for all of the countries, with only reasonable localization issues. It will be advantageous to all if agencies setting accessibility policy draw on each other and use similar language or criteria. In the area of interoperability, however, a higher level of compatibility is required. Interoperability standards must do more than "not conflict," they must also work with each other and allow international interoperability, especially in the communication technologies.

#7 - Ensure that up-to-date information about accessible mainstream technology (AMT) and assistive technology (AT) is available to and being used by the public.

Although most of this report is focused on advances in science and technology and how these advances will make possible the creation of new tools, as well as the need to create these new tools, it is important to remember that current technology is underutilized. This underutilization applies to accessible mainstream technologies and assistive technologies. In some cases this is because the tools are large, costly, or not very effective. Research and development should address these issues.

In other cases the stigma of using these technologies prevents people from using them. The incorporation of these features into mainstream technologies and the creation of better, smaller, less obtrusive technologies will help address these barriers to utilization.

In some cases, underutilization is due to the cost of the products. The creation of newer, less expensive technologies will help to address this issue. Some people with disabilities have no funding source for assistive technologies. Certain technologies might always cost more than most people can afford. In this case there is a need to look beyond the technology to social funding mechanisms. Is accessible technology something that society should provide to people with disabilities in order to improve quality of life? Is it something that society should provide in order to decrease cost to society?

Many times, however, people don't use AT simply because they don't know that such things exist. Currently, most assistive technologies are purchased by people with disabilities or their families. Some do not buy AT because of cost, but a very large number simply do not know that there are technologies that could help them. They are not aware of the features that are already in products they are using that would make the products easier to use. They are not aware of features in products in the marketplace that would enable them to use mainstream products. Retail sales personnel, marketers, and advertisers are usually unaware of accessible features in mainstream products. Assistive technologies exist that would enable certain people with disabilities to garden, cook, write, read, or work, but most people do not know about these products. Information about the products may be on the Internet, and the products may not be hard to find, but most people don't look for them because they do not know they exist. Public service announcements and other mechanisms are needed to inform the public that:

1. Assistive technologies and accessible mainstream technologies exist;
2. AT and AMT can enhance abilities in school, employment and independent living;
3. For seniors, AT and AMT can make life easier, allow people to do more things (or resume doing them), and allow them to live at home longer with less dependence on family members;
4. Many people use AT and AMT;

5. A growing number of assistive technologies can be used fashionably; and

6. There are many places to look for AT and AMT.

If this information is common knowledge among people who have disabilities, their families, friends, caregivers, and medical and health professionals, the use of existing technology and the market for future technology will increase. The natural pressure for products that are more accessible and include built-in accessibility features will also significantly increase.

It should be noted that some types of assistive technology require assistance in selection and fitting by trained health personnel. At present, there is a shortage of individuals who are trained in the effective selection and fitting, and training in the use of, assistive technologies, primarily due to lack of funding. This should be addressed with third party payers, beginning with public payers such as Medicare and Medicaid. Services for which there is reimbursement, and long term market stability, will naturally lead to incorporation of these subject matters in medical and health service programs. This will, in turn, lead to more knowledgeable health service professionals.

CLOSING

Science and technology are moving forward, rapidly opening up new opportunities and posing new challenges. In many cases, they will redefine both the problem being addressed and the fundamental tools to address them. Current solution strategies may no longer work and the current way of classifying things and defining terms may, in fact, need to be reexamined. Since public policy often moves much more slowly, it is very important that, as new policies are created, including accessibility standards and regulations, they are based on functional specifications instead of being technology-specific. We should also move aggressively to capitalize on the new opportunities that science and technology are creating. This is important not only because of the benefit for people with disabilities, but also because of the potential to increase the market for technology products. Where this can be done in a profitable way, the private sector can be depended upon to do this. Studies are needed to identify and quantify those areas that are profitable and get this information to industry where it is not already active. For other important areas, there must be clear and enforced accessibility policy. This policy should encourage all to create accessible products (push), and reward those who practice accessible design (pull) by providing them with a level playing field or commercial advantage. Technology is not the answer to disabling conditions, but it is a powerful, underutilized tool for increasing independence and reducing costs. And, its potential to be a benefit, or to be a barrier, is steadily increasing.

ACKNOWLEDGMENTS

The National Council on Disability wishes to express its appreciation to Gregg Vanderheiden, Ph.D. Director of the Trace Research & Development Center, University of Wisconsin-Madison, for drafting this document. NCD also wishes to express appreciation for the research work of Steve Jacobs, President of IDEAL Group.

REFERENCES

[1]   National Task Force on Technology and Disability. (2004). *Within our reach: Findings and recommendations of the national task force on technology and disability*. Retrieved October 24, 2006 from *http://www. ntftd.org/report.htm*

[2]   *Wireless E-911 implementation: Progress and remaining hurdles: Subcommittee on Telecommunications and the Internet*, House, 108th Cong., 1 (2003). Retrieved October 24, 2006, from *http://energy* commerce.house.gov/108/Hearings/06042003hearing947/print.htm

[3]   Kurzweil, R. (2001). *The law of accelerating returns*. Retrieved October 24, 2006 from http://www.kurzweilai.net/meme/frame.html?main=/ articles/art0134.html

[4]   Kurzweil, R. (2006). *Why we can be confident of Turing test capability within a quarter century*. Retrieved October 24, 2006 from *http://www. kurzweilai.net/meme/frame.html?main=/articles/art0683.html*

[5]   Xun-chi-138-worlds-smallest-cellphone. (2006). Retrieved October 24, 2006 from http://www.mobilewhack.com/reviews/xun-chi-138-worlds-smallest-cellphone.html

[6]   *Samsung breaks new record: Worlds smallest handset announced.*

(2005). Retrieved October 24, 2006 from *http://www.phoneyworld.com/* newspage.aspx?n=1331

[7] XPort® - *embedded ethernet device server.* (2006). Retrieved October 24, 2006 from http://www.lantronix.com/device-networking/embedded-device-servers/xport.html

[8] Sandia National Laboratories. (1997). *New Sandia microtransmission vastly increases power of microengine.* Retrieved October 25, 2006 from http://www.sandia.gov/media/microtrans.htm

[9] Carey, B., & Britt, R. R. (2005). *The world's smallest motor.* Retrieved October 25, 2006 from http://www.livescience.com/technology/ 050412_smallest_motor.html

[10] Svidinenko. (2004). *New nanorobotic ideas from Adriano Cavalcanti.* Retrieved October 24, 2006 from http://www.nanonewsnet.com/index. php?module=pagesetter&func=viewpub&tid=4&pid=9

Avron, J. E., Gat, O. & Kenneth, O. (2004). Swimming microbots: Dissipation, optimal stroke and scaling. Retrieved October 24, 2006 from http://physics.technion.ac.il/~avron/files/pdf/optimal-swim-12.pdf

Kahn, B. (2005). *Printed sensors.* Retrieved October 24, 2006, 2006 from http://www.idtechex.com/products/en/presentation.asp? presentationid=215

[11] Paniccia, M., Krutul, V. & Koehl, S. (2004). *Intel unveils silicon photonics breakthrough: High-speed silicon modulation.* [Electronic version]. Technology@Intel Magazine, 1-6. Retrieved October 24, 2006 www.intel.com/technology/magazine/silicon/si02041.pdf.

[12] Borkowski, S., Sabry, S., & Crowley, J. L. (2004). *Projector-camera pair: An universal IO device for human machine interaction.* Paper presented at the Polish National Robotics Conference KKR VIII, Retrieved October 24, 2006 from http://www-prima.imag.fr/prima/pub/Publications/2004/BSC04/

[13] *The I-tech virtual laser keyboard.* Retrieved October 24, 2006 from http://www.virtual-laser-keyboard.com/

[14] Alpern, M. (2006). *Projection keyboards.* Retrieved October 24, from http://www.alpern.org/weblog/stories/2003/01/09/projectionKeyboards.h tml

[15] Good, R. (2004). Use any surface as interface: Sensitive object. Retrieved October 24, 2006 from http://www.masternewmedia.org/ news/2004/11/25/use_any_surface_as_interface.htm

[16] University of Washington Human Interface Technology Laboratory. Sci.virtual-worlds visual displays frequently asked questions

(FAQ).http://www.hitl.washington.edu/scivw/visual-faq.html

[17] Kollin, J. (1993). *A Retinal Display for Virtual-Environment Applications.* In Proceedings of Society for Information Display, 1993 International Symposium, Digest of Technical Papers, Vol. XXIV. (p. 827). Playa del Rey, CA: Society for Information Display.

[18] Vallino, J. (2006). *Augmented reality page.* Retrieved October 24, 2006 from http://www.se.rit.edu/~jrv/research/ar/

[19] Spohrer, J. C. (1999). Information in places. [Electronic version]. *IBM Systems Journal: Pervasive Computing, 38(4)* Retrieved October 24, 2006.

[20] Taubes, G. (1994). Taking the data in hand--literally--with virtual reality. *Science, 265(5174),* 884-886.

[21] *Andrea electronics headsets.* (2005). Retrieved October 24, 2006 from http://www.andreaelectronics.com/

[22] *Logitech - leading web camera, wireless keyboard and mouse maker.* (2006). Retrieved October 24, 2006 from http://www.logitech.com/

[23] Sensory, inc. embedded speech technologies including recognition, synthesis, verification, and music. (Unspecified date). Retrieved October 24, 2006 from http://www.sensoryinc.com/

[24] Howard-Spink, S. (Unspecified date). *You just don't understand!* Retrieved October 24, 2006 from http://domino.watson.ibm.com/comm/ wwwr_thinkresearch.nsf/pages/20020918_speech.html

[25] LG VX4500 from verizon wireless offers latest in voice command and text-to-speech features. (2004). Retrieved October 24, 2006 from http://news.vzw.com/news/2004/11/pr2004-11-29.html

[26] KurzweilAI.net (click on Ramona!). (2006). Retrieved October 24, 2006 from http://www.kurzweilai.net/index.html?flash=1

[27] Ultratec - CapTel. (2006). Retrieved October 24, 2006 from http://www.ultratec.com/captel/

[28] Wickelgren, I. (2003). Tapping the mind. *Science, 299(5606),* 496-499.

[29] Zigbee alliance -- home page. (2006). Retrieved October 24, 2006 from http://www.zigbee.org/en/index.asp

[30] Myurc.org - home. (Unspecified date). Retrieved October 24, 2006 from http://www.myurc.org/

[31] *The raw feed: New jacket sports built-in GPS*, MP3, phone. (2006). Retrieved October 24, 2006 from http://72.14.203.104/search?q=cache: TB1I942nXQEJ:www.therawfeed.com/2006/03/new-jacket-sports-built-in-gps-mp3.html

[32] Benfield, B. (2005). *Smart clothing*, convergence, and a new iPAQ ::

January 2005. Retrieved October 24, 2006 from *http://www.pocket*
pcmag.com/_archives/jan05/EuropeanConnection.aspx

[33] *The Metlife market survey of nursing home and home care cost* (2006).
New York, NY: Metlife Metropolitan Life Insurance Company from
http://www.metlife.com/WPSAssets/18756958281159455975V1F2006
NHHCMarketSurvey. pdf

[34] Genworth Financial, Inc. & National Eldercare Referral Systems, Inc.
(2006). Genworth Financial 2006 cost of care survey: Nursing homes,
assisted living facilities and home care providers. Retrieved October 25,
2006 from http://www.aahsa.org/advocacy/assisted_living/reports_data/
documents/Genworth_cost_stud y.pdf=

[35] Sullivan, K., & Sorenson, P. (2004). Ease of Use/PC quality roundtable:
Industry challenge to address costly problems (PowerPoint slide show).
Retrieved October 24, 2006 from http://download.microsoft.com/
download/1/8/f/18f8cee2-0b64-41f2-893d-a6f2295b40c8/SW04045_
WINHEC2004.ppt

[36] As we go to press, the U.S. Copyright Office has issued new rules that
authorize the breaking of locks on electronic books so that blind people
can use them with software and hardware that will read the books aloud.
This does not address the problem of book readers that are capable of
reading specific books aloud, but are disabled because of a publisher
setting a "do not read aloud" flag for the book. It would however allow
the encryption to be broken so that a person who is blind could use his or
her own software to read the book aloud. The new rules expire in three
years.

[37] National Council on Disability (2006). *Position paper on access to
airline self-service kiosk systems.* Retrieved October 24, 2006 from
http://www.ncd.gov/newsroom/publications/2006/kiosk.htm

[38] LG VX4500 from Verizon Wireless offers latest in voice command and
text-to-speech features. (2004). Retrieved October 24, 2006 from
http://news.vzw.com/news/2004/11/pr2004-11-29.html.

[39] In Martin v. PGA Tour, Inc., 204 F.3d 994 (9th Cir. 2000), the Ninth
Circuit Court of Appeals held that the Americans with Disabilities Act
(ADA), 42 U.S.C. (sec)12101 et seq., permits a golfer with a disability
to use a golf cart during a tournament.

[40] Trace R&D Center. (2000). Universal design research project final
report: Understanding and increasing the adoption of universal design in
product design. University of Wisconsin-Madison: Trace R&D Center.

[41] Peltz Strauss, K. (2006). *A new civil right : telecommunications equality*

for deaf and hard of hearing Americans. Washington, D.C.: Gallaudet University Press.

[42] Vanderheiden, G. C. (2003). *Access to voice-over-internet protocol ("VoIP")*. Washington, D.C.: New Millennium Research Council. Vanderheiden Digital millennium paper.

[43] Vanderheiden, G. C. (2003). Transcript of comments at the FCC's VoIP forum on December 1, 2003. Retrieved October 25, 2006 from http://trace.wisc.edu/docs/2003-12-1-FCC-VoIP-Forum/transcript.htm

[44] Vanderheiden, G., & Tobias, J. (1998). *Barriers, incentives and facilitators for adoption of universal design practices by consumer product manufacturers.* Proceedings of the Human Factors and Ergonomics Society, 1, 584-588.

[45] http://www.ncd.gov/newsroom/publications/2004/publications.html

[46] National Task Force on Technology and Disability, *supra note 1.*

[47] http://www.ncd.gov/newsroom/publications/2003/adainternet.htm

[48] *National Federation of the Blind v. Target Corp*, 452 F. Supp.2d 946 (N.D. Cal. 2006).

CHAPTER SOURCES

The following chapters have been previously published:

Chapter 1 – This is an edited, reformatted and augmented version of Federal Communications Commission, dated April 2010.

Chapter 2 – This is an edited, reformatted and augmented version of Congressional Research Service publication, Report R40462, dated August 5, 2010.

Chapter 3 – This is an edited, reformatted and augmented version of Department of Justice Statement of Samuel R. Bagenstos before the Subcommittee on the Constitution, Civil Rights, and Civil Liberties given on April 22, 2010.

Chapter 4 – This is an edited, reformatted and augmented version of Statement of the American Foundation for the Blind Submitted to the Subcommittee on the Constitution, Civil Rights, and Civil Liberties dated April 22, 2010.

Chapter 5 – This is an edited, reformatted and augmented version of Statement of Judy Brewer before the U.S.House of Representatives Judiciary Committee Subcommittee on the Constitution, Civil Rights, and Civil Liberties given on Thursday, April 22, 2010.

Chapter 6 – This is an edited, reformatted and augmented version of a Prepared Statement of Steven I. Jacobs before the Committee on the Judiciary, Subcommittee on the Constitution, Civil Rights, and Civil Liberties dated Thrusday, April 22, 2010.

Chapter 7 – This is an edited, reformatted and augmented version of Statement of Daniel F. Goldstein, Esq. before the United States House

Committee on thevJudiciary Subcommittee on the Constitution, Civil Rights, and Civil Liberties given on Thursday, April 22, 2010.

Chapter 8 – This is an edited, reformatted and augmented version of a National Council on Disability Report dated December 19, 2006.

INDEX